TELLING

TELLING

A MEMOIR OF RAPE AND RECOVERY

PATRICIA WEAVER FRANCISCO

A Cliff Street Book
from HarperPerennial

First Cliff Street Books/HarperPerennial edition published 2000.

Designed by Nancy B. Field

The Library of Congress has catalogued the hardcover edition as follows:

Francisco, Patricia Weaver.
    Telling : a memoir of rape and recovery / Patricia Weaver
Francisco. — 1st ed.
      p. cm.
    Includes bibliographical references.
    ISBN 0-06-019291-7
    1. Rape victims—United States—Psychology.   2. Rape victims—
Rehabilitation—United States.   3. Self-disclosure—United States.   I. Title.
HV6561.F73   1999
362.88'3'092—dc21
[b]   98-40614

ISBN 0-06-093076-4 (pbk.)

00 01 02 03 04 ❖/HC 10 9 8 7 6 5 4 3 2 1

For the women, loved and loving

. . . Her soft breasts were enclosed in delicate bark, her hair was leaves, her arms were branches, her speedy feet rooted and held, and her head became a treetop. Everything was gone except her grace, her shining.

—OVID, *Metamorphoses,*
in which Daphne, escaping from Apollo,
transforms herself into a laurel tree.
The laurel leaf becomes the symbol
to honor poets and victors.

CONTENTS

LEXICON

rape–the act of forcing another person to submit to sexual acts, the act of seizing and carrying off by force. [Old French *raper*, to abduct, Latin *rapere*, to seize]

rapacious–taking by force, greedy, subsisting on live prey. [Latin *rapere*, to seize]

ravish–to seize and carry away by force, to rape, violate, to overwhelm with emotion, enrapture. [Middle English *ravisshen*, from Old French *ravir*, to ravish, from Latin *rapere*, to seize]

ravishing–extremely attractive, entrancing.

rapt–deeply moved or delighted, enraptured, deeply absorbed. [Middle English for *carried away*, from Latin *raptus*, past participle of *rapere*, to seize]

rapture–the state of being transported by a lofty emotion, ecstasy. The transporting of a person from one place to another, especially to heaven. [Obsolete French *rapture*, abduction, carrying off]

rapport–relationship, especially one of mutual trust or emotional affinity. [Old French *raporter*, to bring back]

report–an account presented usually in detail, common talk, rumor or gossip, to relate, to tell about, to carry back and repeat to another, to present oneself, to be accountable. [Middle English *report*, from Old French *raporter*, to bring back]

Prologue

WHAT WE DON'T TALK ABOUT WHEN WE DON'T TALK ABOUT RAPE

> The ordinary response to atrocities is to banish
> them from consciousness. Certain violations of
> the social compact are too terrible to utter aloud:
> this is the meaning of the word *unspeakable*.
>
> —JUDITH HERMAN, *Trauma and Recovery*

ONE SUMMER EVENING on the terrace of a Minneapolis restaurant, two women and I unexpectedly found ourselves telling rape stories. Ours. We barely knew one another. The other women were photographers, one on a professional visit from out of town. The conversation turned to my work on this book, and suddenly each had a story to tell: of being raped by a near-stranger in a car, of a date during which clothing was literally torn from her body.

While statistics tell us of rape's pervasiveness—one in four women, one every six minutes—if we've won the statistical lottery, our days begin in the morning and proceed until darkness as if rape did not occur. Or so the story goes. Yet women confess to interior conversations about rape that have an almost tyrannical persistence. Fear, curiosity, anger, fantasy, shame, and obsession with rape form a subtext of presence that belies the absence of everyday conversation about rape.

If the occurrence of rape were audible, its decibel level equal to its frequency, it would overpower our days and nights, interrupt our meals, our bedtime stories, howl behind our lovemaking, an insistent jackhammer of distress. We would demand an end to it. And if we failed to locate its source, we would condemn the whole structure. We would refuse to live under such conditions.

"Myths," said Cassandra Thomas in talking about rape, "keep us from doing the work we need to do based on truth." And one of the myths we live by is that rape doesn't exist. Not really. Not like baseball and heart attacks and love affairs and taxes. Not like the things we talk about together in the evening and feel the need to understand. We don't talk about rape partly because we are bound by superstition. *I couldn't survive it. I might feel differently about sex.* These myths keep women and men from having the conversations that might save our lives, our loves.

In setting down the details of my own experience with rape, I am hoping to start a few conversations. I have done my best to tell the truth, and to acknowledge the layers and distortions that time can contribute to memory. I have not included everything that occurred since August 14, 1981. I've found that the story I have always told myself about these events has a dramatic coherence, that my selective memory has not selected randomly but has kept the telling details, those images that carry the feelings of a whole time.

In the Boundary Waters Canoe Area of northern Minnesota, a precariously thin layer of soil tops the glacial rock of the islands, forcing tree roots to spread out horizontally and creating a fibrous mat beneath the soil. A spark can sink into this layer and smolder underground the length of a whole island before surfacing as a raging fire. During these fifteen years, I have often felt ambushed by such hidden fires.

In 1981, I was a young woman easily pleased, in love with her husband, and inclined toward happiness. After physically surviving a violent rape, that capacity for happiness was repeatedly challenged. Yet, as in all stories relished by the teller, in the heat there was also the alchemy we are promised in fairy tales. As unprepared as I was for despair, it is the dialectic of transformation that remains the deepest mystery. Jack pine seeds, I've been told, only open in a fire.

On the tenth anniversary of my survival, I sat alone in a café, surrounded by women and men who talked quietly, read, stared out the window at the rain. I looked at the faces of the women customers, workers, and owners. Most likely two other women in the café that morning had survived rape. (Researchers estimate a rape-survivor population in the United States of at least twelve million.) The numbers had quietly increased while my ability to talk about my experience had quieted down. I was "over it." I had "recovered." I began to write this book that morning.

I have kept writing because I want rape to be unacceptable, not in polite conversation, but in our lives. (It has taken you perhaps six minutes to read these pages.) I don't want the details of this old story to be kept private any longer. I want a different world for women, for men, and for the children who inherit what we make of it. I want this for you, Andre. And for Julianna, Shawn and Lee, Sara and David and Jesse. For Joe and Cordelia, for Brendan, Molly, Maura, Siobhan. For Sofi and Lily, for Simone, Anton, Maria, Grace, Peter, Alex, Merideth, Mitch, Priya, Olivia, Harry, and Isabel.

I

BEDTIME STORY

THE LIGHT CAST by the red lamp near Andre's bed is too low for reading, so I switch on the glowing globe that illuminates a green and pink world. We arrange ourselves on his narrow bed in the corner, settle down to read Hans Christian Andersen's "The Snow Queen." Andre slouches beside me, willing to nestle close, to let my arm drape around his body as I read.

"Is this going to be boring?" He eyes the thick book, suspicious of the dreamy cover illustration of a girl riding in a golden coach with a huge black crow.

"Maybe in parts," I defer, willing to force this tale on him for my own purposes. There are some words I want him to take in deeply. "This story is told in seven parts. We'll go slow, just a bit at a time. By the end, we'll know the whole story."

"Will it be scary?"

"Only in the beginning."

He sinks lower.

"You know, it's about a girl and a boy who are best friends—like you and Sofi," I continue in the voice of the supplicant. He has begun to resist the books I endorse with my enthusiasm. The bedtime story hour belongs to *him*. "The boy gets lost and the girl tries—"

"Does she find him?" He sits up a bit, resting on his elbows.

"That's the mystery part."

I can see by the way he collapses back onto the bed that I have just responded badly. I ignore him, loving his dear face in the light of the glowing world. I know this story. He is my son, and I want him to know it, too. For "The Snow Queen" is a story of the journey back, rendered as dramatic and harrowing as the event that precipitated the loss. It's a complicated journey, longer than any tale we're used to. The heroine makes mistakes, finds help in strange places, never stops looking for what's been lost. I begin at the beginning.

"THE SNOW QUEEN"
by Hans Christian Andersen

THE FIRST PART,
WHICH DEALS WITH THE MIRROR AND ITS SPLINTERS.

Well, now, let's begin—and when we come to the end of the story we shall know more than we know now! There was once a wicked demon—one of the very worst—the Devil himself! One day he was in a really good humour because he had made a mirror which had the power of making everything good and beautiful reflected in it disappear almost to nothing, while all that was bad and ugly to look at showed up clearly and appeared far worse than it really was. In this mirror the loveliest of landscapes looked just like boiled spinach, and even the nicest people looked hideous or else they stood on their heads and had no bodies.

The story goes on. The Devil's students at the School for Demons try to take the mirror to heaven to fool the angels, but it slips out of their hands and falls to earth, splintering into billions of pieces. Some of the pieces are as small as a grain of sand and fly into people's eyes to make them see only what is bad in the world. And some get caught in people's chests, turning their hearts to ice.

2

TELLING DETAILS

Curiosity is the safeguard, not the death, of the cat.
—SAMUEL BECKETT

BEFORE HE LEAVES my apartment, the man warns that he will be watching. If I tell the cops, he will come back and cut off my nose. I accept, at this point, the possibility of omniscience. When I call the crisis line, a sleepy, kind voice tells me what to do: *Call the police. Call a friend to drive you to the hospital—now.* I do not call the police. Instead I call a woman whom I do not know well. It's an instinctive choice; she lives close, and I sense she can handle such a call at five-forty-five in the morning.

As I wait for her, every moment is marked with possibilities. By the time she arrives, I have run through them all. Can't leave the apartment. Can't risk being seen. Can't stay here. Finally, I run out the front door into the rainy morning with my head lowered, take the necessary risk of appearing in broad daylight.

Laurie's face is a field for me to lie down in. It's all there in her eyes squinting back words, her concentration. She drives. I watch the rain on the windshield, steady, lovely, the shine of it holding me like a child's focus on a spinning ornament. I set up arbitrary races between arbitrary drops, take sides randomly as they wiggle down, win, lose.

At the hospital, a nurse who specializes in treating rape survivors asks me if I have called the police. When I shake my head, she looks at me as if she's about to tell me the most important thing I've ever heard, and she needs to make sure I'm paying attention. *I just want you to know,* she says gravely, *that you're the fourth woman we've had in here this morning.*

Until this moment, I have been living in the narrow, deep space of personal drama. All at once, I understand that what has happened to me, so riveting in its details, so vital and absorbing, is common. The world is full of women who've been through it. Do the math. Not whether but which: which women on the bus, behind the counter selling perfume, singing in the choir, or in your circle of friends have spent mornings like this? I decide to tell.

IN THE EMERGENCY ROOM, I lie on a table to have the deep cut in my left thumb stitched. It hurts. My friend sits at my head and holds my hand. As the clearly nervous intern struggles with the jagged line of the cut, a large worn-looking man parts the curtain and introduces himself as a Minneapolis police sergeant. *You look familiar,* he says to my friend, and she murmurs, *Same thing. Seven years ago.* I crane my neck to see her face, let out a small moan.

Later Laurie tells me her story. While walking her dog by one of our city lakes, she was approached, knocked to the ground, raped by a young man who had killed a woman there several days earlier. My friend escaped, testified at the trial, went on. I hadn't known any of this.

IT WAS LIGHT when Laurie drove me to the hospital that morning, but the events I strain to tell took place in darkness, in the ruined bedroom, down the long hallway, in silence, alone. How did

I get up, pull off the blindfold, put on my glasses, check the digital clock, count minutes, wait fifteen minutes, listening for creaks—the whisper of a sleeve on wallpaper—any sound, rise toward safety, hobble out the door, risk movement, risk existence, grope down the hallway toward dark shapes of furniture, each step thoughtful, life flooding back? Gone, the man gone, not lurking, not waiting, check the closets, in a hurry now, check the front porch, blood draining to my feet, stopping me cold, all heaviness centered low as I see the screen from the front porch window resting casually against the armchair, the wind reckless in the room.

Even as I walked down that hallway, I began to doubt what had just happened, to view it from a distance as if a dream. Not fifteen minutes after the rainy world rushed back to me—cool, gray, noisy, mine—I wondered if I'd conjured up the entire night. I was bleeding, but had it really happened?

This was not the world as I knew it. I couldn't hold myself responsible in the prescribed ways: for being attracted to the wrong person, walking the wrong way in the wrong place at the wrong time. No, I was alone, in my marriage bed, behind locked doors, in a shady old Minneapolis neighborhood just blocks from a picture-book lake where we'd lived without incident or concern for seven years. Perhaps I'd brought this on myself through the force of my imagination, the years of fearing and preparing for just such a night. This immediate sensation of responsibility worked to keep me silent and ashamed for the next ten years.

I BELIEVE IN CONVERSATION, believe in talking things through. I always "tell." I recognize myself in my son when he bursts off the school bus with words on his lips. *Tell me about your day,* he'll say, but first he'll tell me about his. I have not written about rape before. I am interested in why this silence fell, what it cost me and what it bought, the economy of the exchange.

We call it *assault, sexual violence,* but rarely say *rape,* the harshness of the word itself an offense. *It's not pretty.* An acquaintance offers this evasive description of an editorial she's about to have published. I know immediately that it will concern rape. *It never is,* I say, pausing so she will hear in the flatness and the acceptance that I, too, have inside knowledge. But we speak no further. We have worked side by side without knowing, without the possibility of communion.

At first, I could not stop telling the story of the night a stranger raped me. I told it obsessively, sequentially, each detail rigidly in place. I see myself on the blue couch in Laurie's house that first day, telling everything, almost everything, to Deborah, who lies on the floor staring up like someone who has been hit. Three months later I tell my mother not quite everything. My husband hears everything, almost everything, not quite everything, over and over and over. Then suddenly I stop talking. We all take this as a sign of health.

Eventually, I begin to refer to the entire sequence of events as "the rape," thereby not attaching it to myself directly. The critical addition of the article *the* enables me to make note of the event when necessary, without getting personal. Otherwise, when I speak the word *rape,* I feel responsible for introducing pain into the conversation. More than that, I feel responsible for the existence of the word itself. For, if I don't mention rape, it never comes up. Not spoken, it does not occur to us. It *seems* not to occur.

To that first desperate circle of telling, no new names were added. "The rape" functioned as a kind of shorthand I could use with those who "knew." We could breeze by it with a nod, an intake of breath, even if talking in a crowded restaurant. Experiencing rape became a part of my past, no more relevant or necessary to mention than my SAT scores.

· · ·

A DECADE LATER, I open a July 1991 issue of the *New York Times* and read about the deaths of nineteen young women in Kenya during a mass rape at a boarding school dormitory. Although it is, apparently, common practice for women in this part of Kenya to be dragged from their beds into the long grass and be raped, never before had deaths occurred. "Sensing that the boys might attack, all 271 girls sought protection by huddling in the biggest and most secure of the dormitories, a one-story brick building with a corrugated iron roof where 120 girls slept in bunk beds." The male students cut the phone lines and electricity, used large stones to knock down the doors. Nineteen women died in the panic. The assistant principal, a woman, commented: "The boys never meant any harm against the girls. They just wanted to rape."

I feel a whir in my chest like a bird wing against glass. I put the paper down and shut it right out. I speak of it to no one. For if I speak, I will remember. I will remember Richard Speck and the eight nurses huddled under their beds in a Chicago dormitory. I will remember my mother's mysterious warning when I was still flat-chested but hoping for breasts. When in a car with a boy, she said, I must be prepared to jump from the moving car *if necessary*. I began then to rehearse that move, and I'm a bit surprised that I have not yet had to execute it. I have seen the gravel shooting by, the blur of green by the roadside, felt my throat tighten, endured the tension of split-second timing, quizzed myself about how to prepare to jump without letting on to the boy behind the wheel.

I SLEPT NAKED THAT NIGHT. An easy choice back then, but it's hard to remember the person who felt most comfortable on a hot August night with just the coolness of a sheet on her skin. I sat up late in bed, editing a chapter from the novel I was writing, working in a battered notebook with a red felt-tip pen. I remember working well, reaching that feverish place where ideas are coming too fast. I was writing all over the page, turning the notebook to scribble on the margins, pleased with the way a reunion scene had broken open.

I was alone. Alone in the apartment on the edge of downtown Minneapolis, among the old trees and big dark houses full of young renters like ourselves, a few families, and at the end of the block, a group home for troubled kids. My sister had left that morning, returning to New Jersey after a visit. My husband was away for the week, at a photography workshop in the hills of Vermont, elated by the company he found himself in, by the glades and the trees.

I am suddenly full of longing for that young woman. I am writing this in a café across town—a different decade, a different neighborhood, and I am reluctant to let this vision of her go. She's flying down the street on her bicycle, her husband just ahead. They have early tans and French bread in a sack. Just a few months short of her thirtieth birthday, she hasn't been in therapy. She still believes in happy childhoods. She's in love. She writes bright, chatty things in her journal: *Spring begins at 11:03 tomorrow— what news!* The letters her mother has kept from her college years are energetic, taken with every little thing. I'm not sure I'd want to spend a lot of time with her, but I regret her passing. She's about to be lost, and I want to keep her here with her notebook, her red pen, her young body, her happiness.

IN THOSE YEARS, I often slept with a knife under the mattress in the bedroom down at the end of the long apartment hallway. I had nothing particular to fear. The Twin Cities, I would have told you then, was a safe place. The *worst* part of town, I'd say to my friends back in Michigan, is in *St. Paul*. And it's nothing, I'd tell them; a couple of blocks that don't look so good, but *nothing* compared to Detroit. It pains me to recall my voice, smug and naive with its undercurrent of conventional racism.

A formative ambiguity of my childhood was that I learned to love the city of my mother's privileged upbringing: my grand-parents' graceful house on Boston Boulevard, night games at Tiger Stadium, chicken sandwiches at the Detroit Women's City Club. But I also learned to be afraid there, wary on the streets, vigilant about locking my car door when we drove downtown to see the multistory tree of lights across the front of Hudson's department store.

By the time I left, the racial divisions in Detroit had been expressed with violence. In the summer of 1967, the city turned on itself with flames and rage, and the effects of what we soon called "the riots" stoked those childhood fears. I wasn't aware of the economic divisions, the racial dynamics, nor the racism in my associating black neighborhoods with danger. I just knew I wanted to leave. Yet I retained my mother's faith in cities and viewed Minneapolis as a new start, the kind of livable city Detroit had been for her.

So my restless nights in Minneapolis were *my* problem, a troubling weakness caused by my driving imagination and fed by the stories of women I'd known who had been assaulted, mugged, frightened—while jogging, hitchhiking, coming out of a bar, walking into an apartment building, leaning into the backseat of the car to carry out the groceries. I was vague about the details. These things, even among my friends, were not much discussed.

I was vague also about the women in the paper—not up on their self-defense—raped, robbed, beaten—anonymous, unless murdered. I read about them out of the corner of my eye. Afterward, I'd banish them, until they'd emanate out of a night when Tim was working late, and I'd have to enter the apartment alone. Then I'd patrol before settling down, and the stories would rustle like wings, propelling me down the hallway with my useless weapon to check the front door. Yes, locked. Check the door to the basement—yes. Check the windows in the kitchen—yes, locked but open just six inches. Then talk myself down, stop the images, the man at my throat, the blood and disaster.

As I write, my hand steadies the page, and I notice a small scar at the base of my thumb. I am slightly tan, so the milky shine of the scar seems especially bright. They are nearly gone, these traces. My left thumb cut deep, gashes on my forehead, cheeks, neck. I finger the smooth skin below my ear and cannot find the raised line, though my sister says it is visible when I tie my hair back. Over time, loss becomes invisible. There's a wisdom to the mourning cloak, the black, the tombstone.

I am learning not to say *I was raped* but *a man raped me*. Grammatically, this is the difference between the passive and active voice. As I often tell my writing students, the active voice is preferred unless you are trying to hide responsibility.

Out of such semantic sensitivity, the word *victim* has come in for hard times. It is now shameful in some quarters to describe one's life in terms of what is outside one's control. A victim is not a good or powerful thing to be, and *survivor* is the word currently preferred to *victim*. Use of this alternative is possible, of course, only if you have, in fact, survived. There are too many *victims* of sexual and domestic violence who won't be helped by calling them something different. They've literally been murdered. They are *murder victims*. We need that word to describe their situation.

Once we leave the realm of physical survival, there are no simple definitions. It all depends on how you choose to tell your story. *I escaped unharmed* is one way to tell it. *There were no casualties in Desert Storm* is one way to talk about a war. The modifier missing from General Schwarzkopf's famous speech about the war against

Iraq was *American*. There were no American casualties acknowledged at the time he made his pronouncement, though more than
100,000 Iraqis had been killed.

The modifier missing in our use of the word *survivor* is *physical*.
Indeed, my physical body survived, but for a very long time I felt
like a woman in mourning. Spiritual, sexual, and affectional death
is less visible than the death of the body and not necessarily final.
The drama of the burial or rebirth of the spirit is played out in mystery. *I died a different kind of death*, I wrote a month after I'd survived. *I went into hiding and can't be found, not by you, not by anyone. Oh, there are times: on islands or in rainstorms before a fire, sweet
tea, and the poets.* Looking back, these words of mine sound romantic, desperately hopeful, and from the distance of fifteen years, true.
But I would not say it this way today. I am no longer interested in
the death inherent *in* rape. I am interested in the death *of* rape.

Each year for more than a decade, several hundred
women and a few dozen men have gathered at dusk in the
shadow of St. Mary's Basilica in downtown Minneapolis to take
the night back. Three years after I was raped, I joined them. It was
enough to do this march once. I don't draw energy from groups.
For the most part, I felt anxious that night, bored with the
speeches, unsure why I'd come, irritated when I found out that
we'd have to march at the back if I wanted to march with my husband. Men, all of them, made some of the women nervous.

There were a few exhilarating moments when the march
burst through the streets lined with downtown residents, and I
looked into faces I'd been trained to avoid and felt the strength of
the group, the banner I wore making me feel that much stronger,
like a decorated veteran in a Fourth of July parade.

But what was important about that night was *agreeing* to wear
the banner, made from a crudely torn bedsheet lettered sloppily in

red: *I Survived Rape.* Across the park, I stared, oddly shocked and fascinated, as another woman placed an identical banner on my hairdresser. *I didn't know, I didn't know.* I held that banner in my hands again just this morning, and I hate it now as I hated it that evening.

As we prepared to begin the march, a friend emerged from the crowd that had gathered for the speeches and music. She caught my arm to read the banner. I watched her struggle to absorb this fact, which I had never seen fit to mention to her. I saw the puzzlement and hurt in her face, the kind we feel when we fear we are not useful.

WHEN I WOKE IN DARKNESS that morning, a tall figure filled the yellow box of light that was the doorway into the hall. I must have heard the oak floors in our apartment creak, or perhaps there was the loud noise I'd always counted on, the glass, the ripping wood. I am a sleeper who fights waking, who dreams. I don't remember a noise. I woke to the block of light a moment too soon, too late.

He flew through the space between the doorway and my bed. I hadn't translated the dark shape and the broken yellow box when he landed spread-eagled on top of me and my cat. (My vision is so poor I'd have been called blind in another time.) I tried to scream. The sound thickened in my throat like ice. I produced a thin rasp, a strangled cry like a retching animal, and was immediately ashamed. No one would ever hear me, not the woman in the adjoining apartment, not the large and friendly family next door, their windows open to the summer heat.

We fought. The lamp, the bedside table, my books and papers were broken and scattered, though I never left the bed during the struggle.

He had a knife, that was the first thing I understood. The second was that I was going to die there. *This is it?* I managed to protest to myself in the amazing, quiet, huge space reserved for complex thought while all the physical struggle and spiritual acknowledgment of death were taking place. They will find me in a pool of blood, and I will not be able to tell anyone what happened here. I could feel myself getting cut. Suddenly I knew I was spilling lots of blood. I said, *my thumb,* and something shifted.

My voice in the room.

He stopped fighting me and wrapped the corner of the sheet around my bleeding thumb, then patted my torso roughly, as if checking for injury. I knew he would not kill me then. Not that moment. And that was all I needed. One moment could lead to another.

MY MOST DEEPLY HELD BELIEF about my experience of rape is that, by talking, I saved my life. Here's how the story goes: I understood that I would die that night in our bed with the flimsy rattan headboard that gave the room a vague South Seas look. This understanding arrived as a haunting premonitory image. As if from above, I could see my body, blood, the bed. I sensed my own spirit lingering to witness the dying.

As I struggled against the man who had broken into my apartment, I was seized by a regret bordering on outrage. Because I would be dead, I would not be able to tell what had happened to me. Even in those first moments, I felt the press of a future, the desire to sort my death through with those who have always listened to my life: my mother, my husband, and my friends, gathered in a circle as around a fire.

There was nothing familiar or clichéd about those moments on the edge of death. My life did not pass before me in a flash. It took the time it took, but time was altered, becoming deep and broad, my consciousness radically inflated like a parachute, slowing down time by expanding my use of it, giving me access to many levels of perception and interpretation at once.

Then, as I said, an odd thing occurred. As I struggled with the frantic young man with the knife, I knew just as certainly that I would not die immediately. I had a small chance, and it arrived like an opening in traffic. I knew exactly what to do with it. *Tell. Talk about yourself. Spill it.*

I like this part of the story. In fact, I have become committed to it. In this part, I look cagey and victorious and well worth saving. But is this Scheherazade or was Scheherazade this? Was knowledge of that old story the source of my impulse, or do we instinctively tell stories to save our lives?

THINK OF THE CHATTERING, scheming, list-making inner voice of soul turned way up—so loud you don't recognize it as your own, so calm and brilliant you think of angels. I knew that my task was to listen to this voice and to perform perfectly. It removed panic and any need to weigh alternatives. I knew exactly what to say and do, moment by moment, at the level of muscle tension and tone of voice. I began to concentrate. I lit up like a room-size computer in a 1950s horror movie, lights blinking, wheels turning. *On.*

This voice—calm, steady, certain—is the spiritual heart of what happened to me that night. Since then, I have heard the voice often, as a flicker in consciousness, a whisper with innate authority. *Don't answer the phone. Leave now. Don't go yet. Call her today.* Such are its mundane instructions. And when I do not listen, I feel connected to the story of Judas.

I'VE TOLD THIS STORY many times. I've never told it this way before. Telling requires a kind of courage that I normally lack. This book is an exertion, a promise I'm keeping, and it's slow going.

. . .

I REMEMBER FLYING HOME to tell my mother, three months later, so heavy with dread on the flight to New Jersey I felt certain we would fall from the sky. I lied to my younger sister about the reason for my visit and was unable to tell her the truth for two more years. I chatted the evening away with an astonishing false complacency.

The next morning my mother and I were alone, and I found it impossible to speak. We were at the kitchen table with coffee cups, and she knew I had something to tell her. She was looking at me as if she couldn't imagine what would rob me of my words. I felt I was carrying a bomb. Every time I told someone that I had been raped, I caused a small explosion. (I didn't use the word at this point. I was still saying *assaulted, attacked.*)

I didn't want to do this to my mother. I actually considered not telling her, despite the plane trip and the knowledge that the dreaded therapy group back in Minneapolis would be waiting to hear the outcome of my visit. Nothing seemed worth the explosion I was about to set off in her. Then she guessed. I've never figured out how she knew. She said only that it was suddenly obvious, there in her consciousness, as if written before her. Everything flowed from this. We talked all morning. I have almost never loved her more. She listened and did not interrupt. She let it all be true and did not fall apart.

SINCE I WRITE BOOKS, people often ask, *So, what are you working on?* It's a touchy question under any circumstance, requiring the writer to articulate what is rarely clear in a work in progress, namely, what the thing is about. These days, I find myself sizing up the questioner then answering bluntly—*I'm writing about rape*—or evasively—*I'm interested in exploring the subject of sexual violence.* I'm often aware of causing discomfort, of the conversation collapsing into embarrassed silence, and wishing in those moments I'd kept quiet.

When my questioner is a woman, I'm likely to be *told* a story. It may be a story that's never been told or a story that hasn't been told in a long, long time. I've come to believe that rape survivors are encouraged to keep their long silence by a kind of societal magical thinking. *If we aren't talking about it, maybe it isn't happening.* But it is also true that we've been given little help in listening to the stories women tell. Without context, these stories startle us, lay us low, deliver us to a state of despair. Under such circumstances, we may ask *not to know.* Survivors hear the request for their silence, and can be left believing they are the problem and their silence the solution. While the women keep quiet, get over it, move on, and put it behind them, the rapes go on and on.

H<small>E REACHED INTO</small> the small dresser on the left side of the bed and emptied the drawers onto the floor. He grabbed my swimming suit and made it into a blindfold. Although I spent the rest of the night unable to see, my memory of the rest of the night is visual. I have asked anyone I thought might have an answer how this is possible. When the detectives announced that the rapist was experienced, had left no fingerprints, had apparently worn gloves, I said: *Yes, tan leather gloves, driving gloves with those radiating lines of little holes across the front.*

I can accept that I experienced an explainable psychological phenomenon whereby my knowledge of the house, my imagination, and my visual memory combined to create remembered scenes. However, I have a new tolerance for weeping statues, apparitions in cornfields, and sightings of saints. I understand how literal we are, how we're organized to explain our experience, whatever its source, as physical reality.

. . .

I BELIEVE I SAW many things. I did not "see" the rapist's face. I find that curious. From his phrasings, his voice, a scrap of visual memory, I have made a picture of a young black teenager. Several years later, at the grocery store, I thought by the sudden, violent clutch of my body that he was, in fact, bagging my groceries. As he walked me to my car, I chattered like a robot, hoping to keep the conversation going long enough to recognize his voice. But in the daylight of a winter morning, there was nothing I could prove.

How much money do you have? he asked. I told him about the forty dollars in cash in the next room. He made me stand, and we took the first of several stumbling trips out of the bedroom. We walked to the back room, where he emptied my purse, took the money and my driver's license. I *see* this. He holds the card up to the light in the hallway, reading my name out loud. *What does the* M *stand for?* he asks. I remember thinking, *He's making conversation.*

Once again, I decide to talk. More accurately, I feel advised to talk. *Talk, tell, everything. If he's thinking about killing you, which he still is, let him know just exactly whom he is killing.*

It stands for McKee, I say. *It was my grandfather's first name. It's Scottish.* I'm friendly, light as a feather. In this moment, I enter into a relationship with someone who wants to hurt me. Later, I will tell him things many people don't know. Answer questions others have never thought to ask.

3

TELLING DETAILS / 2

Leaving the bedroom has calmed me. As he steers me
from the back room to the bed again, I ask him his name, casual, as
if I'm simply interested, though instantly he knows I'm trying to
trick him. He shoves my face down into the bed. Hand at the back
of my neck, hard. *Shut up.* It's the voice of someone who could kill
me, and I'm back to not knowing whether I'll live past this conversation. All I've got are words, and he's got them, too.

We talk about money again. He needs more money.
Don't I have any more money?

In the bank, I offer, regretting it instantly, unsure suddenly of
the line between accommodation and idiocy.

Where's your bank? He's excited. *Is that your car out there?*

Yes, the Volvo, the old, yellow Volvo. I ache to take the words back.
I've just offered my car, my bank account. *But it's the middle of the
night. The bank's not open,* I rush to point out. I'm grateful for a
thought that doesn't send me down the river. He's too strung out,
young, or confused to ask for the keys or to get me to sign a big check.

He seems disappointed but drops this line of questioning in
favor of convincing me that he really needs the money. He needs

the money, you see, because he's got bills. He can't get a job. There aren't any fucking jobs for someone like him. He needs to get more money from me tonight.

Then, silence—a pause for emphasis—*This is my job*, he declares. I sense a slight apology, like the doctor muttering that it might hurt a bit. No, no, that's not quite it. He's feeling sorry for himself. He sighs painfully, and I am lost, stranded without words or a moral compass. I'm the fish on the line, and a man's gotta eat.

Doesn't he?

Doesn't he?

I BEGIN TO TALK. I talk about not having enough money, about living close to the edge. I launch into a monologue about having to sell my record albums on the street during college for food money. This was not, in fact, true. I *knew* people who did this. My roommates and I often let a small group of street people eat and sleep at our apartment. No matter. He's just surprised enough to hear me out before pouncing on the word *college*.

You went to college? So, your parents have money then? He knows there's money here somewhere.

No, not really, I want to say. I worked in college. I scraped garbage off plates in the freshman dorm, waited tables, scrimped. My father spent his best years feeling under the gun, struggling to keep the ship, and all three college-age kids on it, afloat. I mourned the impossibility of attending the school of my choice. *Can't afford it*, my father snapped, dropping the glossy catalog on the table. There was never enough money it seemed, never a sense of ease. I do not mention the silver vegetable dishes at the dinner table or the yard of pines and hardwoods stretching back to a creek, the comfort we took for granted. I say nothing. There's no way to bridge the economic gap between us, nothing I can say that does not sound suspect in this room.

What's your father do? Where'd you go to school? What did you study? he prods, probably not in those words. I have lost all but the harshest of his phrasings, cannot recall his voice or the patterns of his speech—only his threats, the killing in them.

*J*OURNALISM, I SAY, and we talk that over for a while. He's interested, in a vague way, as if passing time. I tell him I'm writing a novel. He reacts much like anyone I've ever told. Really? he says, surprised, somehow more pleased to be talking with me than he was a moment ago. So what's it about? He asks questions. How long have I been working on it? Do I know anyone in real life like who I'm writing about? Do I have a publisher? He is particularly curious about publishing: How does it work? Do I pay the company to publish the book or what?

We are talking in a dark bedroom with the wreckage of our struggle all around us. It's raining, perhaps four-thirty in the morning. I'm naked, blindfolded, lying facedown on a bloody bed; a stranger, whose face I never see, is somewhere behind me in the room. I am angling for his heart of gold, a heart I envision simply because he's listening to me. What saving grace is there for me in the powerful listener I can't seem to live without?

Nothing in my fearful imaginings of rape has prepared me for this intimacy. Conversation, for me, is nearly as sacred as lovemaking. My intimate relationships are all founded on talk. It's what I know of safety, acceptance, trust, and affirmation. As a result, I regard this kind of scene in film or onstage as clever artifice, poetic license providing an opportunity for deep character revelation. But this is my life, weaving itself into a story I have a hard time believing.

T*HERE ARE PERIODS* when the voice in my ear directs me to remain silent. I have no idea where the man is or what he is doing during these times. In the blind dark, my terror builds. I say, *Please don't hurt me,* very quietly, hoping his voice will be a kind of sonar, locating him. He pounces. *Shut up.* Shoves my head down. *Or I'll cut your nose off.* Danger clangs around the room. A child has grabbed the wheel of the plane. There's a snake in the shower. The air raid sirens are blaring and you can't reach your loved ones. *Act right.* Again and again that phrase. *Act right and you won't get hurt.* Years later I hear it in my nightmares: *Act right.*

Was this the moment when he delivered the sentence that bound me for so long? *Now you'll have something to write about,* he sneers. Never, I resolve in that moment. Not one word.

GET UP—he's yanking on my arm—*we're going for a walk.* He steers me down the hallway toward the kitchen. Blindfolded, I stumble into the walls. I *see* myself here, hunched, broken in the yellow hallway light, groping my way forward. Nearly a year later, my mother will remark on my posture as I come off an airplane. She'll watch me closely the whole visit, alarmed by this change. I'm unaware that I carry my shame so visibly and wonder in what other ways I resemble the prisoner when my defenses are down and my sadness has me collared.

He wants a beer. I feel the relief of the hostess that I have some on hand, the relief of the prisoner that we're in the realm of food and drink. It's an odd domestic moment. I wonder if he's going to stay all night or forever. I can live with that, I decide. I can live with anything.

Years later when a Tibetan friend explains her ability not to dwell on sadness or difficulty, she says that being born human is such a triumph, the culmination of thousands of lesser incarnations, that bad days are just never that bad. "I'm grateful not to be a fish," Sonam says. Yes. I'm open, at this point, to any kind of deal that this young man wants to make. It's not for years that I will understand that there is a price for bargaining with your humanity. I hate what he knows about me.

He's careful to keep his hand on me, dragging me like baggage to the refrigerator, rummaging around with one hand. I *see* this—see the shine on the cans. He's got the knife with him; I feel the flat of the blade against my arm, steering me. He talks. I don't remember any of his words. I'm exhausted, trying to keep up with the shifting mood, trying to listen, to anticipate, and now, shivering in the kitchen, trying not to be seen. He is so relaxed that I indulge in a sense of a future. Perhaps no more harm is going to come to me. Later, when the police pronounce him a professional, I understand that we were just taking a break, relieving his boredom.

When we return to the bedroom, he tells me to lie down, and then he is silent a long time. He sits next to me on the bed, close, near my head and drinks his beer. He also smokes a cigarette, possibly a joint. The police found burnt matches on the floor, but I have no memory of smell. He is silent for so long that I become terrified. Not the panic or the adrenaline clarity of the first terror, but a slow, frozen, cynical knowing, an engulfing certainty that now is as good a time as any for killing. But I understand in the long silence that he will rape me first. Until this moment, I have not considered the possibility. I feel foolish, a little slow or stupid. *Of course*, I say to myself in the quiet. I feel him waiting for the knowledge to settle in, as if this is exactly what he wanted. How he'd planned it. He relishes the moment as he drinks his long beer. This is the hour of my acquiescence, this silence and all that it contains.

4

TELLING DETAILS / 3

As I write, I rise from my chair and circle the house. I kick the walls and the refrigerator. I shout, and my cat lifts her head, unaccustomed to this kind of outburst from me. I feel like a giant. My body tingles with power. When I tell this part of the story, I see in the flinch of the listener what is wretched about subjugation. Normally, I do not feel it. I am a calm narrator without opinions. Today I am my own audience. I react by wanting to do damage.

I'D ENTERED a yawning, dark, featureless time, intolerable in its lack of definition but preferable to whatever was going to happen next. I have always hated total darkness: a power outage, a cave, a haunted house. In darkness I cannot declare an intention, cannot plan, can only imagine.

My sister survived a fire as a teenager. In the hallway of the house on fire, smoke smothered the available oxygen and created a blackout. She describes the darkness as a tomb of concrete, describes a sensation of being buried alive. Darkness usurps power. This is knowledge we share.

Perhaps it is here that I developed the acute hearing that later became such a hindrance. My only clues in this darkness are sounds. Beer sloshing in the can. Flimsy book matches scratching across the floorboards. An abrupt inhale on a cigarette or joint. The clanking of his belt buckle as he takes off his pants.

There is such hatred in the slowness of this, in its indulgence. The conversation that I believe saved my life may also have given him confidence. He'd sized me up, too, found me desperate to live, willing to bargain. Someone who was not going to cause trouble. From the safety of the future, I look back and wish myself a warrior, defiant, refusing to engage.

I ACTUALLY REMEMBER LITTLE in my thoughts and feelings about the physical experience of being raped. I remember in my body the subjugation of my body. *Just get through this*, I tell myself. I know I might be killed, but at this point, I believe I will survive. *All you have to do is get through this.* It is so dark, and I am so tired and afraid. The easiest thing to do is to leave. Let my body stand in for me. As I write this, it sounds like a decision, but it happened instinctively, as one swerves just soon enough to avoid the crash. These are not willed acts of survival. We are in some way assisted, led away from what can only harm us.

I remember this moment from a spot up near the ceiling, through a consciousness separated from the bodies below. As a result, my memory has a quality of dreamy calm that I want at times to rip away. Only years later, when I learned to retrieve a bodily memory of this night, did I finally experience some of the details.

Here is what I do remember: I remember the sound of his belt buckle, unmistakable and final. I remember knowing from that sound that he is standing at the end of the bed. I remember waiting for him to be human with me and knowing by the silence that he will not be. I remember a sense that this is ritualized behavior, prescribed, a matter of necessity, of course, of pride.

I remember that everything happens in agonized silence. It seems we are both in pain. In the air is a charge akin to the weight that descends when one enters a great religious place, a solemnity I'd expect in the chambers of an execution or just before a duel. I felt a hint of this in the church when I married and later when I was in labor: a sense of brushing up against the fundamental, the sublime. But as this stranger prepares to rape me, there is no beauty. Were I to paint this scene now, I would include the angels, gathered in the corners as in the great cathedrals. But in the darkness, I am unaware of such protection. I feel abandoned to the company of evil.

I remember the moment when he puts a pillow over my face. The beloved sister of a beloved friend had been murdered this way, smothered by a stranger with a pillow. Death reenergizes me. I raise my arm and cautiously place it between my mouth and the pillow, breathing shallowly through this small act of defiance. He keeps the pillow over my face during the rest of the time his body touches mine. He does not want to see me. He wants a body without a head attached, leaving me a head without its body. I keep busy up near the ceiling, thinking about maintaining breathing room under the pillow, about contingencies, what to do if I feel the knife on my neck or his fist on my face.

He enters my body with his body in a sad and quiet way. He is unable to maintain an erection. I lie perfectly still and then begin to wonder with detachment and clarity what the best strategy might be. Is he going to remain inside me until he ejaculates? *At this rate, it will take all night.* Should I come back into my body, try to speed up his physical arousal? I consider this remarkably difficult option for quite a while before rejecting it. I won't cooperate. Somehow I know it will haunt me into my future. I don't remember anything else, just silent, fruitless movement, and then he rolls away and lays beside me for a long few moments.

There is emotion in the room at this point. Sobriety, sadness, perhaps belonging to both of us, a brief connection I never want to acknowledge. He is invisible to me and I to him. We do not communicate with eyes or spirits or voices, but our bodies have come together, have met.

There's an avalanche of sadness behind such a meeting. Rage can be summoned to keep this load of sadness at bay. Women are beaten, killed, tortured, stabbed thirty-nine times with an ice pick. It did not happen to me, and I was allowed to rise out of that bed toward a future. But a part of me stayed behind, and the mark of that deep disappointment, that close contact with depravity, remained. I was not afraid in this moment. I remember thinking that he was.

LIFE BEGINS AGAIN in the bathroom. He wants me to take a bath, and I know this is a bad idea, though it's not until a doctor examines me for evidence that I understand the reason. *Why don't I just wash up, a sponge bath?* I suggest and am elated when he does not object. Things are moving quickly. There's been a slight shift of power, as if he's been caught off guard and is suddenly a young man in a stranger's house, going along with her suggestions.

I feel as if I saw everything in the bathroom, though I'm quite sure my blindfold was still in place. The light is on. I lean over the old claw-footed tub, reach for the natural sponge resting near the wall. *See* his gloves. I take the sponge and turn on the water in the sink. I pat my body with the sponge, lightly, a charade. This passes inspection, and energy floods through me from being allowed this much control.

But he leads me back into the bedroom and orders me to lie down once again. It seems obvious what is coming. *Please don't hurt me.*

Shut up!

He shoves me down. I cannot summon the energy to act. It is raining, cold. I hear him rummaging around on the dresser top. He is stealing my Russian box, my watch, and bracelet, but the only precious object I visualize in this moment is my opal necklace. A gift from Tim, I can't bear the thought of losing it, can't say a word about it.

Don't move, he says. *Keep your head down. If you call the cops, I'll come back and cut off your nose.* It's not an expression; it's an intention.

All right, I say, fervently, ready to swear to anything. *I promise. I won't call.* He seems to be listening. I've got words and I say them all. *I won't call. I don't want any trouble. Won't make any trouble. I won't call the police. I don't like the cops. There's no phone in the bedroom anyway. I just want to be left alone.*

He repeats again that he will know if I have called. He will know. And he will come back. *Act right,* he says. *Writers need discipline,* he says. He slams the words in my face. Then he walks out of the room and closes the bedroom door.

I listen. I listen. I can't hear anything. I listen to degrees of silence. Hear rain. Hear silence. I am alone with my thoughts. I don't know what to do, alone with my thoughts. Nothing I know is of any use. What will happen next? Anything. What can I do? Best not to do anything. I concentrate very hard on not moving and on not making a sound. I want him to forget I'm here. I don't want him to think I am thinking.

This is a state of mind to which I will return, perhaps for the rest of my life, when propelled into fear. I'm wild with desire to know whether I am safe, but at the same time paralyzed by the possibility that I am not. Paralysis with adrenaline is a shattering combination.

I do not know how long this state of animal alert lasted, but at some point I stepped out of my hypervigilant monitoring of sounds to have an abstract thought. *I can at least take the blindfold off.*

I've LOST TRACK of my glasses, tossed somewhere during the struggle. I narrow my eyes and peer at the digital clock on the table by the bed. The fractured red—*5:30*—is as sharp in my memory as the confettied sunlight on the water out the window where I write this morning. I decide to wait fifteen more minutes before doing anything. How did I pass those minutes? I do not remember.

I do remember clutching my chest to find my opal necklace hanging around my neck. It's a triumphant moment. *You didn't get this!* I think, as if I've succeeded in thwarting him. I swing my legs out of bed, locate my glasses on the floor, stand, and creep toward the door.

The decision before me opens and opens. Should I look out into the hallway? Should I walk out into the hallway? Should I hide? I have been allowed to live because I have promised not to leave this room. This is the logic of the prisoner. I've made a deal I'll be expected to keep.

Perhaps he is just on the other side of the door, testing me. Perhaps he is coming back soon, and I've squandered my only opportunity to escape. There is a doorway between these two alternatives. There is opening the door or not opening it. Taking a step or remaining frozen. Finally, the possibility of escape drives me out the door.

The hallway looks as it always did, normal and quiet. I stand still as a trespasser and try not to breathe. After a few minutes, I can see beneath the skin of the hallway. Can see it quivering. I detect a pulse, a beat, the vibration of danger. The quiet, normal hallway is a *similacre*, the woods without tigers, the ocean's unbroken surface without the sleepless sharks circling below. You can't out-wait a shark. No matter how long you stare at the surface of the ocean without seeing a fin, you can never step in without considering its presence.

I make my way down the hallway. Each step takes me closer to danger or to safety. It's paradox I've learned this night. Paradox and a new set of rules. I no longer am fascinated by Patty Hearst. I only feel for her, for the cruelty of being caught in this paradox twice: forced by her captors to learn new rules, punished by her rescuers for having learned them so well.

When I reach the kitchen and the doorway that branches out into the dining and living rooms, I have a wide view of what used to be my life. I rush toward it without caution. There is the table, scratched and majestic. The plants pawing at the window, the gold-leaf mirror Kathleen and Julie gave us for our wedding. The old milk can painted orange. There is the soft armless chair and ottoman in front of the window where we take naps with the cat, the wicker chair we bought for five dollars in Ann Arbor, the wooden telephone cable spool Tim refinished for a table. Look at it, look at it, look. Listen, listen, look, listen. Don't look too long without listening. He could be in the closet, inside the oven, on the back stairs, in the front hallway . . .

. . . where the door stands ajar. The front door was bolt-locked last night when I went to bed. How did he get in? I worry this around for a terribly long time before hitting an actual thought: he didn't get in—he went out. Out. He has left by the front door. My mind in these ecstatic minutes feels like a slot machine played by a desperate gambler with a strong right arm. Thoughts revolve, bounce off one another and occasionally line up so that I can proceed. As soon as I realize that the rapist has gone out the front door, I close and lock it while continuing to consider the possibility that he is still hiding in the apartment.

I rush around. I feel as if I've been pulled down a narrowing tunnel toward a point of light. When I reach the pinprick of brightness it floods over me and the walls dissolve, and I am swept into such a crowded place. Like a tourist strolling along the Ramblas, I can hardly decide where to look, what to touch first. I look at everything, claim the smell of the rain in particular, woody and clean, stirring up the smoky stink of asphalt. I come back into my body enough to recognize that I have crossed over. I am lucky, lucky. I am spinning. I am on my knees.

I walk out onto the screened-in front porch with caution, aware that I am visible here from the street. I am still supposed to be in the bedroom. This movement into life is privilege and transgression. It takes me a few moments on the porch to realize that the breeze is too strong. Another moment to see that there's a gaping hole in my house. I hold on to the chair against the dizziness caused by this collision of one world with the other. I finger the screen that's resting against the overstuffed chair, trying to grasp what is already dissolving into dream. The screen takes on a magnified aspect, and I touch it as if it were something rare, impossible, a relic. So that's it. He came into the porch through the screen window. The French doors to the living room were open. He walked down the hallway, changed my life, drank a beer, and left by the front door, which he did not bother to close.

*I*NKY DARK *when he hits the sidewalk, but the dawn lifts away the press and shelter of darkness. He can hear traffic on Hennepin Avenue, the roar of the freeway just beyond. A car rolls past him, kicking up rain.*

Dizzy with images, he needs something, a way back. He walks quickly down the sleeping block. Inside the houses, some are stirring, pulling up covers against the unexpected coolness. Others are rising to distract themselves with morning radio, to stand in the shower and worry about the day.

He moves past them all like a snake into underbrush, to a house nearby, possibly to the bus, into the arms of a woman, to the comfort of a drug or the culture: a slasher film on TV, a porno magazine, music videos.

By midafternoon he sleeps, sated, his sleep an arid oblivion from which he wakes full of the old restlessness. Hungry. Before he hits the street again, he catches a glimpse of his face in the small mirror over the sink as he rinses the meanness from his mouth. Keep moving. Business to transact. Dump the box, pawn the gold. Move through the streets like a man.

5

CARRIED AWAY

It was very sad, the things men carried inside them.
The things they did, or thought they had to do.

—TIM O'BRIEN, "The Things They Carried"

HE CARRIED AWAY the six opalescent blue beads I'd
bought in Ann Arbor in hopes I'd make a necklace someday. They
lay scattered about the bottom of the Russian lacquer box that he
also took away.

He stole the gold bracelet made from my grandfather's watch
chain. It was constructed without seams—a quirky jeweler's chal-
lenge, my mother always explained. My grandfather had the broad,
flat chain made into bracelets for his three daughters, whom he
loved in a quiet way and whose later sorrows, I suspect, would have
puzzled and confused him. My Aunt Eleanor gave me her bracelet
in one of her many unpredictable acts of generosity. I don't remember when it came to me, but I was young enough to invest in its history, old enough to listen patiently to the explanation of its genius
(no seams). I came to love its soft burnish, the color like tea, and the
way it announced itself quietly on my wrist as the real thing.

I have trouble recalling a single specific moment in my grandfather's presence but for the eerie exchange late in his life when he
told me in great detail of his dinner at 10 Downing Street with

Winston Churchill. My grandfather was in the early stages of senile dementia, and though he had never even been to England, he could recall the flavor of the cigars they had smoked after dinner. I carry his name as my middle name, and I loved him as I might love a hillside in the sunlight. He *was*, and he was connected to me. The bracelet made it so, even after my grandfather's death.

HE CARRIED INTO MY HOUSE the violence he could no longer carry. He carried himself lightly and with practiced ease. He took my faith and my grandmother's gold watch, the one I'd had repaired just days before at the cluttered little shop on Lyndale Avenue.

I saw my father's parents once a year, and I never developed a sense of comfort around them. First-generation German immigrants, they were hard-working, quiet people. My grandfather bought a hobby farm during the Depression, anticipating the possible loss of his job. Instead, he worked all day at Westinghouse Air Brake and taught himself farming at night by reading books.

My father remembers a mother who never complained, kept the floors clean enough to eat off of, baked and canned, loved company. My memory is of a tiny woman who kept her head down, sent cookies packed in peanuts every Christmas, a woman in whose rare laughter one glimpsed a wary child. Shortly after her death, I received a package from my father containing some costume jewelry and her watch—plain, gold-plated. I didn't wear a watch or have much of a relationship to time, so it was just the thing.

A few days before it was stolen, I took it to a little shop I liked because it reminded me of old downtown Detroit. The windows were painted black halfway up, JEWELRY REPAIR reversed in white letters. The jeweler shuffled back and forth behind the low counter, reaching into tiny boxes for parts, muttering over miniature tools. White-haired, taciturn, he told me he'd engraved the date of the cleaning on the inside of the watch. An odd, irrelevant mark of pride I'd thought at the time.

Later, I recalled this fact with pathetic joy. The world made sense for a brief moment. Like in a novel, this would be the clue that would lead to the return of my watch and the arrest of the man who'd taken away what I believed about justice.

THE RUSSIAN LACQUER BOX, where I kept the beads, the watch, and the bracelet, was a gift from my parents for my graduation from college. Rectangular, perhaps six inches long, its glossy black sides were finished with a band of gold filigree. Made in the village of Kholui, these boxes are painted according to tradition with an egg tempera, a demanding medium that necessitates a nearly perfect execution of the image the first time. The technique dates back to the painters of Russian Orthodox icons and is still practiced in only a few villages.

On the cover of the box was a painting of the Snowmaiden, a young woman in an ice blue greatcoat. She stands in a winter wood under a thin moon. Stars appear to be caught in her cape, and on her head is a jeweled headdress reminiscent of an Indian goddess. At her feet, nearly indistinguishable from the snaking limbs of a pine tree, is a fearsome bearded spirit. The Snowmaiden has paused, tilting her head to listen to the spirit's whispered message.

According to the Russian folktale from which the image is derived, the Spirit of the Wood has been sent by Spring and Winter, the Snowmaiden's parents, to deliver a warning. It is time for her to make her way into the world, yet they fear that Yarilo, the Sun God, will glimpse her and cause her death. They have consulted the Spirit, who now comes to deliver his advice. "You shall be safe from death by the sun's rays so long as the love for a man does not enter your heart."

The Snowmaiden spends her days indoors, staring out the window at the other young people. Late one day, when she can no longer bear the isolation, she puts on her cape to join the others and meets Lel, the shepherd boy. He plays his flute for her. Despite her joy, she returns to the cottage, afraid of the price of these feelings. Spring comes to the village. The young people gather to dance, and the Snowmaiden becomes sadder and sadder. Finally Lel begs her to join him, and she relents, renouncing her immortality. "Play for me, dearest Lel. Play one last song for me," the Snowmaiden cries tragically.

I DIDN'T KNOW this story when my mother gave me the little box. I was charmed by its miniature beauty but not thrilled. I was hoping for cash or a television, perhaps. But it grew on me. I carried it with me when I left home. It was an object of grace and quality, something to start with, something to aspire to. Not until I was turning forty, when the Snowmaiden came back to me, did I learn the story of the frozen woman, locked away in the name of protection.

These are the things he carried away. How they came back is another story, for what was stolen returned eventually on a tide of determined love.

6

AFTER

> Traumatized people suffer damage to the basic structures
> of the self. They lose trust in themselves, in other people,
> in God. . . . The identity they have formed prior to
> the trauma is irrevocably destroyed.
>
> —JUDITH HERMAN, *Trauma and Recovery*

LATE AUGUST on Lake Superior, the fourth day of a rainy, slate gray week. I write in a shed just up the sloping hill from the rocky shoreline. I have written much of this book near unbroken horizons: the Gulf of Mexico, the Great Lakes, the Boundary Waters of Minnesota. The steady push of waves lifts my sinking spirits.

Today, when I walk out on the rocks and try to feel a sheltering sky, I am disappointed. The lake is having a fair-to-middling day, no surging, no fire. The rocks are wet and burnished from a morning rain, and the sky and water meet without distinction. Moss and lichen rise in relief against the rocks. The green looks saturated, as if it holds its own source of light, the ochre tasty, intensifying to orange.

But it isn't enough. I feel alone and empty of desire.

And then I see it—long and square, moving steadily along the horizon. An ore boat. Humans! I stand taller on my rock, stretching toward this appearance. I feel oddly excited, connected to the sailors I imagine pacing the deck of that huge ship gliding past me in the *gloom. I'm surprised by how passionately my heart attaches, longing for its own, despite my disappointment, my deep need to resign.*

Eventually, I dressed and reopened the front door of my apartment. I held my breath. I hadn't yet learned that breath permits awareness. And in awareness is safety. At this point, I still believe I am safe if I follow orders, if I play dead. After this night, I work at not drawing attention to myself or the fact of my aliveness.

The woman in the apartment next door lives alone. I knock hastily, loudly. I knock again, turn away, and notice that the front door of my building stands ajar. Rain is coming in. But I cannot run down the few steps to the entryway to close the door, and I cannot afford to be out in the open any longer. I draw back into my apartment, lock the door, and sink to the floor.

My breath comes in great, heaving pants. I need to stay low. I duck under the bank of windows running the length of the dining and living rooms, remain invisible to those who represent love or help or safety.

I decide to *call* my neighbor, hoping the telephone might wake her. But what is her number? What is her last name? I am as clumsy in directing the movement of my thoughts as my father, years later, trying to direct his hand following a stroke. I sit on the floor, stare at the newly refinished floorboards—shiny, the color of wheat, stall out for several minutes.

My neighbor's name rises like a piece of flotsam on a wave. I crawl toward the phone book. *If you call the police, I'll come back and cut off your nose.* Can he tell the difference between a call to my neighbor and a call to the police? It isn't safe to make *any* call. I scurry into the coat closet, dragging the phone on its long red cord into the pile of boots, umbrellas, vacuum cleaner attachments, and hats on the floor. Sitting on the floor, I listen to the telephone ring a long time through the wall between our apartments.

Who can comfort me? I rehearse what I might say to each of the other four tenants in the building. In the process, I realize that what has happened to me has a name. A stranger has raped me. I stare at the blood caked along the gash in my thumb and realize that comfort is not what I need. I call the Rape and Sexual Assault Center in Minneapolis and ask for help.

BEGINNING WITH this phone call, my story takes a turn toward privilege and luck. Eventually, I became aware of what I was spared: death, disfigurement, beating; the complication of knowing the man who raped me, of being married to him, of being his daughter; the pressing, buried pain of recovering in isolation; the transforming shame of an indifferent or punishing family. Instead, my return to health was *because of* rather than *in spite of* other human beings.

A WOMAN I'VE CLEARLY WOKEN with my call asks pointed questions and directs me to the hospital. At the top of my list of regrets is the fact that I ignore her instruction to call the police. I have heard enough survivor stories to know that my choice tells you as much about me as about the situation. I talked and I listened and I did not disobey. In this way, I stayed alive. But what were the consequences of my *continued* silence?

The few minutes that it takes for Laurie to drive to my house are anxious spaces that cannot be filled. I cannot bear to be alone and wretched for another moment. I fear time and the knowledge that begins to arrive. I see myself in the mirror through the eyes of shock. *Who is this poor woman?* Her face is cut in many places. Her neck, her arms, her hands, her chest—cut. Her eyes are empty. *Where have I been while all this happened to her?*

Staring into the bathroom mirror, I scare myself. I scare everyone who sees me these first days. *I* scare them. I can't escape the feeling that this is my fault. I've lost the race I've been running all my life, and it's proof of some fundamental last-ness, base-ness: I am no better than this. I am wretched. I am hated. *I* am. There is no separation between the experience and the responsibility. When you win a race you *feel* like a winner. I understood that I had lost.

Those who could see through this confusion with their love or wisdom became heroes to me. They taught me, eventually, to see through it myself, to refuse to be a carrier.

I HAD NEVER BEEN to Hennepin County Medical Center and would never have chosen to go there. As the downtown county hospital, I expected it to be the facility of last resort, with a long wait, perfunctory treatment from a staff inured to suffering. Instead, I was given exactly what I needed by people whose kindness seemed schooled by experience. I have since heard versions of this first, important contact in which women are dismissed, labeled, shamed, processed. I can speak of the difference it made to be cared for at this time. The nurses and doctors seemed to know I was bereaved. Their voices were hushed. The lights were dimmed. Men and women looked directly into my eyes with gravity and offered help.

The Sexual Assault Unit of the emergency room was a separate, quiet place where the first order of business was to persuade me to call the police. It was here that Laurie brought me, here where the nurse on duty told me of the three rape survivors they'd treated already that morning. If I called the police about "the incident," as she called it, I would not be charged for tests or services. The county would assume the costs.

Something broke inside when I heard this. From here forward, each time someone joined me in knowledge or action, it was as if a rope had been dropped over the cliff, offering a way up, a way out. The fact that the community would assume responsibility for my medical costs brought me back to the notion of a world I could belong to: a group gathered at the top of the mountain, furious enough to pay.

Years later, a fourteen-year-old friend who had survived a rape confided that she knew her attacker. She was reluctant to testify against him, to be responsible for sending him to jail. "You don't have to take that on," I said, remembering with acid sharpness that first moment when my private nightmare met a public response. "That's *our* job," I said, casting my hands wide to indicate the neighborhood, the grown-ups who lived there. "Just tell the truth." I knew it was not so simple, but I recognized her relief, remembered the restorative power of not feeling left alone with a problem I had not created.

IN A PRIVATE ROOM, a nurse collects vaginal swabs for evidence and to determine whether I have contracted a venereal disease or am pregnant. These tests are routine. The idea that the results will define my future is not routine. The *future* is not routine. I have just been delivered from a deep focus on the present moment struggling to establish the next moment. These tests are, quite literally, my awakening to the notion of the future. I remember just wanting to curl up, to be left alone. And I remember my silence on the examination table. *Act right*, he said. The nurse was quite calm about it all. Of course, it was not her future on the slide, in the little vial of blood.

As I lay back in the thin cotton gown under the paper sheet, I let myself imagine the possibilities. *Venereal disease:* madness, illness, contagion, contagious, premature death. Didn't they have drugs for that now? *Pregnancy:* the rapist's child, abortion, grief, the body's subjugation continued, impossible. These days, fear of HIV would overshadow both.

Years later, I heard a story of a woman who bore the child of a violent rape, despising the infant with an intensity she could not have predicted and later coming to love and care for the child. My imagination is drawn to that story, for in its images is the transformation toward which I struggled.

THE TESTS ARE PERFORMED by a female nurse, but at some point a man comes in with a camera, explaining that he needs to take photographs of my wounds for evidence. He is perfectly respectful and quiet about this, but it requires that he label each cut with a small white card lettered with my name and a number. As he props these cards next to my arm, neck, face, hand, and methodically photographs each, I feel myself disappearing. I lie on the examining table, silent, trying to stay perfectly still, to make myself an object, to cooperate and wait for it to be over. Gradually, this compliance does me in. I leave my body again.

I have not survived the knife attack but have been murdered in my bed just as I'd envisioned. Once again, I hover over my body, this time in the morgue as the remains are being photographed, stark flash pictures to be slid out of a manila folder and shown to my husband when he comes to identify my body. The association is exact, an odd metaphorical moment I experience rather than recognize, when the fate I've only just escaped lingers and presses in on me, asserting its parallel existence and its possibility.

AFTER MY THUMB was stitched, Laurie drove me back to her house on the other side of Lake of the Isles from my apartment. Perhaps we talked. Perhaps I began right then to tell her the story. Perhaps. I remember quiet, nothing asked of me, nothing required. I remember scrambled eggs and strong black tea.

Her husband was in Turkey for several weeks, and the strain of her own remembered pain as she witnessed and ministered to mine was considerable. Later, as she talked about her recovery, I glimpsed the fearsome dimensions of the journey back. Because the rapist had attacked her out of doors, she was unable to walk her dog or even stand in line for a movie without panicking. She eventually responded to aversion therapy. Accompanied by a therapist, she took on troublesome situations again and again until she was able to learn a new response.

It was from Laurie that I received hope. That morning she looked as healthy as any woman I'd ever known, and I carried that image with me into the uncertain years of my own transformation. "At some point," she told me the first night among the plants and polished oak of her upper rooms, "it becomes like a book on a shelf. Every once in a while you take it down and look into it again." It would be years before I stopped reading the world through that experience every day. But that first night, when we slept in her big bed so that I would not be alone, it was she who lay in the dark and cried.

THE DETECTIVE from the hospital shows up soon after we've eaten breakfast and immediately agrees to fix Laurie's parking ticket from the hospital. I like him for that and for everything else he does. I am disappointed about what he cannot do. I have an impression of him physically—large, calm, smart, a wide soul from knowing so much about humanity in extremity. He could have a role in any TV cop show of substance.

I give him the broad outlines of what occurred. This is the first time I tell the story in detail. During the next few days, each time I tell it, the events will belong to me alone a bit less. I feel connected to each person who listens, so it is no surprise that I feel a connection to this man, who might be the fabled cavalry, coming to my rescue. He never says, *Just leave it to us*, but he doesn't have to.

W HEN HE ASKS ME to accompany him to the apartment to search for evidence, I panic at the thought of police cars and uniformed officers arriving at my apartment building. I am still completely brainwashed by the rapist's threat to return. He listens without judgment and promises unmarked cars and plainclothes detectives.

Our building is a modest 1930s fourplex in a neighborhood between downtown Minneapolis and the most meditative of the city lakes. Several blocks away, the rental property dries up and the houses grow, culminating in Lake of the Isles, where the grace of the homes is as easy on the eyes as a woodland. I love living this close to the city, in the slipstream of elegance, a reprise of my grandmother's life in center city Detroit half a century before. Now, as I hurry up the cracked sidewalks, head down so as not to be seen, not ever again, I feel that the greatest loss is of my neighborhood. The fear seeps into that first return and every subsequent one.

To this day, I approach the building with trepidation. The lake, the shops nearby, the physical world I inhabited for seven years, has nearly ceased to exist. While it looks much the same in actual fact, I avoid the neighborhood so assiduously that it has all but vanished. On the rare occasions when I make an always unplanned turn off Hennepin Avenue and plunge into the dark, cool streets where I used to live, the air remains charged with my fear. The building seems to carry a remnant of what occurred there, and I wonder if its occupants struggle with troubled dreams.

· · ·

THE POLICE found nothing, though they opened their black cases full of fingerprinting apparatus and appeared to search diligently, dusting the shiny surfaces, collecting the spent matches and cigarette butts, asking me to lead them spatially through the events of the night. These men seemed not to enjoy their work nor to forget that the evidence they collected represented the end of a world for the woman who stood before them.

When they could find no fingerprints—not on the brass doorknobs, the porcelain tub, the refrigerator, the dresser, not anywhere—the detective in charge of fingerprinting sighed and proclaimed that the man was a professional, had clearly worn gloves, and they packed up their powder and their little black bags. I never heard from them again. They didn't say, Sorry, lady, but this happens every day, and we just don't have enough to go on here. They didn't say, Don't call us, we'll call you. I watched the detective's big shoulders moving out the door. I'm sure he didn't mean to let me down.

A decade later, in an eerie reminder of my own experience, a dozen rapes again occurred in that neighborhood. The police failed to pursue the connection between them, failed to investigate aggressively until public pressure compelled action toward the arrest of the "serial rapist." The community was surprised and briefly outraged by the lack of attention initially given these cases. I was outraged but not surprised. What is the difference between a *professional* rapist and a *serial* rapist? Public pressure. What causes the public pressure? Media attention. What determines which professional rapist will be *called* a serial rapist by the media? In 1981, there were 461 reported rapes in Minneapolis and St. Paul and 138 attempted rapes. By 1993, those numbers had risen eighty-seven percent.

• • •

I KNOW WHAT I WANT. I want a box in the newspaper every week—perhaps a little map—noting rapes, attempted rapes, batterings. I want the information I need to get the lowest rate on my credit card debt *and* the information I need to stay alive. I want signage. In Minneapolis, we have Department of Transportation signs alerting us to the fact that we are entering an Accident Prevention Zone. The signs show a merry little tow truck carting away a cartoon car and are intended to remind us to drive with caution in areas where accidents happen frequently. I want Rape Prevention Zone signs funded by the Department of Public Safety. That's what I want.

I FIND MY CAT crouched way back among the pots and pans in a little-used recess in the kitchen cupboards. I imagine she's been there since she flew from the bed and felt the air charge with danger. From here on, I regard her as my familiar, a protective being, the only one who knows what I know.

Stranded momentarily in the kitchen, I remember that I've scheduled a lunch with a friend today. The impossibility of this simple comfort comes as a small, solid shock. It is, I realize with difficulty, a Friday afternoon for most people—lunches, meetings, peanut butter sandwiches for their kids. Others are immersed in birth and death. For those immersed in birth and death, the things with which we occupy ourselves look like popcorn to the starving.

When Tim was once seriously ill, the small talk in the restaurants where I waited for the crisis to pass was nearly unbearable. When pregnant, I experienced this sense of transcendence not as fury but as smugness. In a meeting with serious adults, the important drama was hidden from everyone but me. But this day, the fact that I could not have lunch with my friend caused neither fury nor self-righteousness. It kicked off grief. Perhaps this is the nature of operating in a state of shock. We move out of numbness one feeling at a time and each emotion remains distinct and exaggerated in impact. I longed to be the woman who would have written a bit in the morning, done the dishes, rooted about in her box of earrings for something to flash at her ears, dashed out into the rainy afternoon for soup and laughter. She seemed a lost world away.

As I imagine telling my friend what has happened, my sense of responsibility deepens. In charge of delivering information, I become its author. I consider not telling. I don't want to burden her. Don't want to ruin her day. The desire to "protect" another adult from knowledge is always a mislabeled self-protection.

In much the same way, I later struggled with a desire to protect my son from knowing that I had experienced rape. I wanted a different world for him, one that looked like the room we so carefully prepared before his birth, its walls the blue and rose of an evening sky. A world absent the Holocaust. A world in which the Chinese government did not murder its Tibetan friends' quiet countrymen. This impulse stems from a notion, conservative at heart, that we are limited, that we require for our happiness the blindness that passes for innocence in children. But I've come to believe that evil is best borne when it's fully visible. In knowing it, we know complexity. And from complexity comes possibility.

Luckily, I'd been given a friend who knew this already, who knew I was at the beginning of everything that comes after. Deborah drove directly across town. She lay on the floor in Laurie's house and listened to the whole story, staring up at the ceiling. She told me I was brave; she told me she loved me and was glad I had not been killed.

She took me with her to where she worked in St. Paul because we both knew I could not be alone. She told me that she'd gotten other news that day, about a writing student who had committed suicide. She told me this in flat sadness because I was her friend and she, too, was carrying grief that needed to be heard. I heard it as a train in the distance, a call that reaches you, somehow personal though it does not belong to your life, a sound that reminds you there are others journeying.

In Deborah, I was given a friend whose fierce heart cleared a space large enough for my pain and so, like a tourniquet applied tight and soon, stopped the bleeding. She poured coffee for months; she made tuna sandwiches; she never asked me to stop talking about it; she never said put it behind you. I find this something of a miracle. I've known this capacity in few other human beings, and I do not believe, though I take friendship seriously, that I have it myself.

The essential difficulty of any grief is that you are alone with it. We have not much practice, outside of our experience with art, in entering the emotional reality of another. Self-pity begins in this loneliness. *No one understands how hard this is.* A skillful illusion that the pain is shared can be a bridge to beginning again. This requires a listening infused with love and anger. A friend whose heart has many rooms can hold you up out of the water.

I DID NOT WANT to tell Tim, either. As strange as this sounds to me now, I had to be persuaded to call him at the photography workshop in Vermont. I argued against it, as I recall, on the basis that he would know sooner or later, but if I called him right away he would have to leave the workshop he had looked forward to for so long. Why not wait a few days? I'm not sure out of what exact tangle of hopes and fears this conviction arose, but I do know that it carried no weight with Laurie and Deborah.

It took him less than twenty-four hours to return, and I was desperate for him by the time he arrived. That first afternoon in Laurie's kitchen, I couldn't see the extent of my injury. I was a fire walker, invincible because I had no feelings at all. The cuts began to throb when the shock wore off, and so did my need for the person with whom I felt most loved.

We'd been married seven years. We met when I was a junior at the University of Michigan. He drove up on a motorcycle one day to visit his friend who lived in the front of the house in which I lived at the back. I was on the porch with my roommate, and I remember stopping in midsentence to stare at the man on the motorcycle. As he took off his dark glasses and helmet and gazed back at us, curious merely about the sight of strangers on the porch, I felt my soul stake a claim.

We married two years later and lived a lucky, loving life together before the stranger raped me in 1981. We are divorced now after twenty years of marriage, and there is no doubt in either of our minds that the demands of that violent disruption got the best of us. Much of the story of what came after is the story of a marriage, of the bounty of human love and its limits.

7

EXODUS

It strikes me now that one of the untold burdens of the survivor
of rape is what she has come to know. She has been left holding
the truth. It is not only a threat of death she has encountered.
That threat has carried with it a malevolence and an insanity with
a long history. . . . For her the world has changed. And in this
understanding she is isolated, because for us who have not been
raped the world remains the same. We keep the fact of rape at the
periphery of consciousness and do not let it bear on our vision.

—SUSAN GRIFFIN, *Rape: The Politics of Consciousness*

AT THE MINNEAPOLIS/ST. PAUL AIRPORT the next
morning, people stared. Fresh cuts on my face, neck, and hands
whispered some kind of story. But the staring barely mattered. As I
waited for Tim's plane, I battled a sudden breathless desperation.
Years later, in labor with our son, I felt a similar weakness during the
period between the promise of painkiller and its actual arrival. In
both cases, the anticipation of relief came over me like a swoon.

I remember that moment in the airport, but today I have
been unwilling to write of it. I've been staring out past the thrash-
ing of a northern lake, reluctant to recall the depth of my connection to the man I needed more that day than I have ever needed
another. We have lived apart three years as I write this, and still I

hearken back to our marriage as a time when life was as it should be. Melancholy arises at the prospect of setting down these memories. Loss, longing, mystery.

But that day, the mystery lay *outside* us. In the love between us, there was safety and sanity, a chance at making sense of what was shattered. I knew the moments and movements of his face as one relies on a daily landscape. Yet the world had so turned around that his appearance there on the airport walkway felt miraculous, as if he, too, had returned from the dead.

In the hours that followed, we exchanged stories, understanding at some level the need to bridge a gap. We had each experienced a reversal of reality, and we had experienced it alone, our accustomed support system—each other—out of reach. He told how he had walked the fields in Vermont and wept. How he was driven to the airport in someone's Jeep, bouncing along in the company of men he had just met.

Two summers later, on the second anniversary of my survival, we returned to Vermont and the fields that roll out broad and green in that high country, white barns in the unbroken sunlight, a gallery of photographs incongruous in an outbuilding. Walking there, I had a glimpse of how startling and intrusive my phone call must have been. We had both been changed that day.

I don't remember our conversation. What I remember are his fingers on my face, tracing the curve of my neck, tentative and shaking across the skin of my right hand, dabbing a pungent comfrey salve on my cuts. At some point on the ride to the airport, a man named Carlos had handed him the jar to bring to me. It would prevent scarring, he said. I have it still, its label gone dark from the oil of its contents, its flowery script nearly fifteen years old now.

Still with me as well is the tenderness of those moments of silent ministering, Tim's fingers touching the evidence of an event he struggled not to imagine. It contains nearly everything I have to say about how we moved from that moment forward, all the love, the inadequacy, and the mystery of what became our new marriage. We didn't know then that our original marriage had ended. But the touch of his fingers, fearful and loving on my face, and the faith we invested in a salve to prevent scarring contain the best of us, and also our folly.

THOUGH WE CONTINUED to stay with Laurie, we returned to our apartment to see "the scene of the crime." Despite the fact that I'd been back with the detectives, it was only when I walked up the stairs with Tim, coming *home* this time, that I saw what had happened there.

When we entered the bedroom, I saw the bloody bed. Iron brown stains in blotches across the sheets had soaked so deeply into the mattress we had to throw it out. I saw the remains of the wooden lamp over the bed hanging at a crazy angle like a broken limb. I saw my papers and books tossed about and torn like refuse, mixed up with the wreckage of the bedside dresser. I'd never seen anything like it, not in a TV movie nor in my imagination. The sight depleted me, and I sunk beneath a cresting exhaustion fueled by hopelessness. We would never clean this up, never make it right. We would not be able to live here again.

I SIT TODAY at a pine table by a window where glass panes open wide like wings and look out at the sleek black sinew of water moving past. In the distance is the sound of hammering, men repairing the structures on this island where I have come to write. There are only women in residence on the island this week, and we are joining in the work of restoring a small cabin perched out over the water so that the light at sundown dances on every wall. At dinner, we women and these men laugh until it grows dark.

I am afraid here only of bats and mice and the spiders that sashay across my bedcovers. The day and its night, the men and women, the spirited loons calling out *loneliness, loneliness,* these things please me. Yet, when I sit down to write, I am pulled away toward a dark knowledge. I'm tempted to work at forgetting, to let the past go.

My point is how difficult it is to take my eyes off the sky to describe the eyes of the woman who came to clean the blood off the floor the day that Tim and I returned to the apartment. She worked for a cleaning service owned by a friend of ours. Upon hearing what had happened, our friend offered to take care of cleaning the apartment—a remarkably perceptive gift. The woman who volunteered to do the job had herself been raped at some point in her past. She did not expect us to be there when she arrived.

We'd left the door from the hallway open, and she walked in tentatively, calling *Hello?* as we emerged from the back bedroom. We stopped each other cold. She let out a gasp. She was not happy to see me. Though Tim was in the room, the focus shifts in my memory to the two of us staring at each other across the dining room table.

I was suddenly horrified at the whole idea. Why was she cleaning my house, my bloodstains? She stammered, seemed unable to meet my eye. I was hard to look at during those first days, but I believe that my presence also obligated her own memories. That afternoon, I felt angry at the woman whose presence required me to *see her,* and I believe she was angry about having to look right at me.

It is easier to gaze out this sunny window and imagine a world at peace with itself than to look at these memories. I resist, and you who are reading may want to resist. Why go into it then? There are a million sad stories and only one day like this, balmy and just right, a woman's infectious laughter and the steady beat of a hammer in the near distance. Why talk about rape when it makes everyone uncomfortable, including the remarkable woman who cleaned my apartment that afternoon? Why not just go on hoping tomorrow will be a better day?

Because perfect days are built on difficult mornings. Tomorrow will look exactly like today—*one every six minutes*—until, at the very least, we tell one another the truth. "Self-destruction is a great and morbid bitterness in which one destroys what one knows by destroying oneself," wrote Andrea Dworkin. The impulse not to see is a powerful undertow that keeps us all in danger.

As I remember the look of that room, I am pulled toward the slough of grief where I rarely let myself go. *The end of a world*, I want to say, then feel overly dramatic. A small world did end there, and I can barely stand to hover over the battleground.

Before we left the apartment, Tim asked me to kneel in front of the bed with him and pound it with my fists. I resisted, hating this sort of exercise, and watched him, impressed by the blows he was beginning to believe had been his responsibility to inflict. Many conversations those first days involved Tim's distress that he had been gone and my gratitude for his absence. I felt that my survival had depended upon careful acquiescence to the crazy man and the knife, and that Tim's likely aggression would have ended in his own injury or death.

Years later, while listening to testimony during a rape trial, I came to accept the possibility of effective confrontation and resistance. I regret my inability to grant this truth earlier. Not only had circumstance denied Tim the opportunity to help me, but I was unable to give him my faith in the *possibility*.

WE LIVED at Laurie's house for the next three weeks, sleeping in the unfinished third floor on a spare mattress. Laurie's husband was still in Turkey, so we became a sort of temporary family, sharing meals and walking together in the evening. Those weeks are recorded with the luminous simplicity of childhood memories—a few vivid details that dissolve almost into nostalgia.

Each morning Laurie ate a piece of whole wheat toast with peanut butter and drank a glass of grapefruit juice before going to work at the plant store that she owned. For three weeks I did the same, taking a childlike comfort in accepting the routines of another as my own. Instead of going to work, I spent my time staring at the vigorous plants that filled her high windows. I'm certain I did other things as well, but the essence of those first days is visible in the immense amount of time I spent staring at plants.

The ferns in particular occupied me, as did the flowering begonias that Laurie grew to resemble roses. I needed the sunlight as I needed food and air, so I would pull a chair right up to the window, getting as much of my body into the light as possible. I remember being aware that I was not thinking. I was a rock, neutral, as if dosed on morphine, absorbed by tendril and petal. I had lost the world of men, but it seemed I could be transfused by the elemental world.

I can still do this. I have just gazed long into the birch trees out my window, the leaves twirling in the smallest breeze, and beyond the yellowed green of birch, the dark forms of pine and the wash of sky. I believe I gained this capacity to lose myself completely in a field of color, or regained it from childhood, during those weeks by Laurie's windows. The difference is choice. In those days, I could do nothing else.

AFTER A WEEK of rest, I, too, returned to work, as an assistant editor at a magazine and a writing teacher in residence in schools around the state. I began to tell a few people outside my immediate circle what had happened and made a list in my journal of the flowers, notes, and prayers that came my way. It's curious how few of the names listed there were close to me then or are now. Tim's response and the reaction of intimate friends were critical for regaining my sense of returning to the fold, but recognition by others also had power.

In studying war veterans as well as survivors of rape, incest, and domestic violence, Judith Herman, author of the pioneering book *Trauma and Recovery* observes, "Restoration of the breach between the traumatized person and the community depends, first, upon public acknowledgment of the traumatic event, and second, upon some form of community action."

For soldiers returning from war, we have medals, monuments, parades, holidays, and public ceremonies of memorial. With rape, the criminal justice system functions as the formal arena for recognition and restitution, and has largely failed at both. Survivors must gather these elements of repair in their own way. I was given every blessing in this regard, and still I struggled to make my peace. It is a measure of how difficult this task can be. For centuries women have coped with rape trauma in hiding, in private, or faced the unimaginable difficulty of being held responsible for the crime. I am sometimes amazed that the world's women can function at all.

Expressions of sympathy and outrage from others were the first rung on the ladder out. At a work-related conference that September, I greeted a woman I had not seen all summer. *How are you?* she asked breezily. I looked at her directly and let her know without specifying that something serious had occurred. *I'm sorry,* she said, *but you'll be all right. You're a rock.* I remember thinking, *Yes, I am. All I do is stare at plants.* I have since come to understand how important direct assurances are to the drowning. *You will be all right. You are strong. This time will pass.* They become resting places where we stand to gather strength. They don't need to be elaborate or elaborated. We're in no mood to question them, and logic cannot diminish their power.

Similarly, there is great comfort in simply restoring the physical connection between oneself and others. I had to learn this, since it is not my way. I learned it from a group of friends I knew only socially, a group characterized by their high spirits and verbal jousting. Tim and I participated in a yearly croquet tournament put on by this group, distinguished by dress whites, a champagne brunch, and competitive silliness on the course.

A few weeks after I was raped, we were invited to join them for a practice game near the rose gardens bordering Lake Harriet. I was reluctant to go. I was unclear about who knew what and did not want to take on such a difficult subject with this group, largely made up of men I did not know well. But we did go, and we did play croquet in almost total, placid silence. I have never seen this group so quiet before or since. No one spoke of what had happened to me. I could never have guessed how soothing it was to be with others who, by their lowered voices and energy, indicated they knew I was in pain, but did not speak of it nor require anything from me.

My natural impulse when I am in pain is to isolate myself and to lick my wounds alone. One of the pleasures of knowing this group has been learning how those inclined toward community celebrate and mourn. The point of the croquet game seemed to be that we were gathered together in one another's presence, occupied in an activity that, by its distracting and communal nature, offered comfort. We didn't talk and talk, as I am also prone to do. We didn't pretend nothing had occurred, although an outsider might perceive it to be so.

This strikes me now as a particularly midwestern, particularly male, form of connection. Fishing in silence is the basis for a friendship. Fixing a car together is a close personal encounter. The croquet game touched me deeply and did its work. I can still hear the quiet tapping of balls, the hushed voices and long silences, and see the late afternoon sunlight streaking across the grass.

The exceptions to these kind responses had a terrible power. Several women friends were simply unable to discuss rape, so my attempts to establish a connection with them were subtly but definitely blocked. This disturbed me until I understood how consciousness of rape can threaten a delicate equilibrium built on denial. If one's fear is high enough, one cannot afford such a conversation, cannot afford to let rape sit across the table. It needs to be way across town, belonging to others, to those on television, to foolhardy women, to someone nothing like you. I learned to forgive the women who could not hear me, but this was the beginning of my learned silence as well.

Only one man reacted with cruelty. *You look fine,* he said, with a snort of surprise. *I thought maybe you would have grown horns.* At the time, I was completely unable to respond, but his remark dislodged a dark stone of shame that had been forming in my gut. Kept at bay by the men and women who had supported me, it was now set free to loom and grow, attracting the particles of fear that are free-floating in the culture, gathering toward a potent charge of self-hatred.

*F*EELING *IS* MISSING *from my days and nights,* I wrote toward the end of the first month. It's possible to say such a thing in a single sentence, but the burden of wading through the days without any feeling challenges my descriptive abilities. Virginia Woolf captures a moment from earliest childhood with this remarkable image: "The feeling of lying in a grape and seeing through a film of semi-transparent yellow." Though she ascribes positive associations to this memory, my sense of separation and diffusion is evoked by her image better than anything I can compose.

I especially felt no anger, except at problematic targets: innocent bystanders, Tim, the heat. I was most angry about the fact that we had lost our ability to live in our apartment. This led to my stubborn insistence that we spend a night there to explore the possibility of returning permanently. Whatever Tim's true feelings, I do not remember him objecting for long. Two weeks after the rape, on the day I had my stitches taken out, we returned for the night with an almost romantic determination.

Is it any surprise that the night was sleepless and tortured? I have memories of childhood summers in a muggy room with no fan and the gray inky sea stretching before me as I toss and sweat and struggle to lose consciousness. This night was a similar agony. Hot, brutally conscious, my new extrasharp hearing tested for the first time, I spent the night listening for small sounds of warning, magnifying them into adrenaline-charged alerts, shaking Tim awake or sitting bolt upright in bed, paralyzed by predictions I could not voice, waiting for what surely must come next, never sleeping, hating every image I could conjure up of the apartment, refusing the memories that were triggered and triggered in exhausting rounds of shutting out thoughts only to have them arise again.

In the morning, we discovered that a screen had been removed from the back bedroom window though entry was blocked by our window locks. Who had done this and when? I could not say for certain that the screen had been present the morning after the break-in, but I suspect that it had. The possibility of an attempted second break-in was enough to seal our mutual desire never to sleep in that bedroom again.

And we never did. I have a black-and-white photograph that Tim took of me lost in an afternoon nap, sprawled across that bed with its rattan headboard salvaged from one of Tim's commercial production sets. Our cat, small then, sits in the window. I look at the young woman sleeping there and do not know what to say to her. She appears foolish to me and blameless. But her happiness is a truth I have built a life on. She sleeps in that bedroom where we spent the simplest years of our marriage. She expects that life will not change. She considers herself complete, including the defects of character she laments in her journal. She wants nothing more than to finish the novel she has written in fits and starts during the last four years. She believes it will be the hardest thing she will ever do.

Years later, as I struggled to live with fear and sadness, I believed that recovering from rape was the hardest thing I would ever do. We are larger than we imagine, and we do not imagine future pain if we are wise. We recognize it and prepare to meet it, but in those moments of rest when our task is to sleep dreamless, we are wise not to quantify our pain. I am, just now, learning to live alone, to live without my son for days at a time, to search for solace and meaning outside the marriage that defined me for twenty years. I will tell you that this is the hardest thing I have ever done. But I take some comfort this time around in the image of a young woman asleep in her bedroom, dreaming of a book, her husband in the next room chopping vegetables for supper.

Once we decided that we could not return to our apartment, we were out of luck in a big way. Laurie had opened her heart to us, but it was not without its toll. Her own recovery had been long and demanding. I now realize that seven years is not a reliable measure of anything. It may be enough time to let the memories become, in Laurie's words, "a book you put on the shelf." On the other hand, my situation had forced her to open the book and keep it open.

A week into our stay, her husband called from Turkey. As I passed the room where she sat, I saw her gripping the phone as if in desperate need of his presence, and then from the next room I heard her telling our story and sobbing. I stepped out of myself for a moment and recognized how difficult it might be to experience her own feelings as she took on the task of supporting us, alone. I knew we needed to find a place to live.

• • •

During a conversation with the administrator of the writing program in which I taught, I reluctantly told him that I had been raped. I was, essentially, justifying my inability to meet a deadline. I felt particularly awkward because I did not know Jim well, and he was my boss. In addition, I'd already noticed the difficulty that men had in responding to this information. The silent croquet game occurred partly because the men involved were speechless.

But instead, this conversation was a door that opened into an enduring friendship. When I hung up the phone, a curious sensation of relief, almost joy, replaced the apprehension I had felt. Jim's ability to hear me, to ask questions, and to respond had deep roots. Perhaps that is why he was able to offer me, from that day forward, exactly what I needed: a male friend willing to listen and not wish me silent; respect for what I had brought to the situation rather than a judgment about its occurrence; a loving tolerance for how I'd been harmed and an ability to appreciate the new facets in me that resulted. Therapists refer to the need for "integration," a vision of oneself that includes the traumatic event and its effects. Jim's steadfastness through the many years it took me to integrate rape helped make that possible.

Later, as I came to know Jim's work as a poet, I realized that he was, simply and always, articulate about emotion. Yet in addition, he had the ability to hear *this*. Conversations about rape between men and women are particularly strained and restricted. The exact nature of the threat that rape as a *subject* seems to pose for men is a question that needs men's attention. Coming to terms with this discomfort is one of the most important steps men can take to change the atmosphere of violence between men and women.

It's my impression that, faced with the subject of rape, men tend to scramble for a foothold. In conversations about this book, for example, I'll notice a hesitation, like an intake of breath. Do I blame all men? Am I angry with or afraid of men? These are understandable questions, not unlike those I have when a person of color introduces race into the conversation.

Thoughtful men wrestle with a generalized sense of responsibility, but the discomfort this causes can effectively deter further thoughts. A common strategy is to assign rape to a group of matters called "women's issues" that don't require male attention. At a party when the conversation turned to a series of highly publicized rapes, I noticed that all the men had left the room.

One man acknowledged that the subject forces to mind ancient locker room conversations and ongoing fantasies that, by definition, objectify women. Suddenly the ground feels shaky. Sexual responses that fall easily into the realm of the normal are up for scrutiny.

"Consent can be mushy," offered another. In fact, I would suggest that confusion about consent haunts every conversation about rape between men and women. We are moving away, awkwardly, from the assumption that "nice women don't say yes, and real men don't listen to no." Much fun was made of the 1993 Antioch College Sexual Offense Policy, which defined consent as "the act of willingly and verbally agreeing to engage in specific sexual contact or conduct." But at least this guideline paves the way for an easy joke between men and women who are attempting to have these conversations.

This scene from *Until Someone Wakes Up*, a play about date rape written by Carolyn Levy in collaboration with college students, considers the riddle of consent.

Waiter: Would you like some coffee?
Woman: Yes, please.
Waiter: Just say when. (Starts to pour.)

Woman: There. (He keeps pouring.) That's fine. (He pours.) Stop!
   (She grabs the pot; there is coffee everywhere.)
Waiter: Yes, ma'am.
Woman: Well, why didn't you stop pouring?
Waiter: Oh, I wasn't sure you meant it.
Woman: Look, of course I meant it! I have coffee all over my lap!
   You nearly burned me!
Waiter: Forgive me, ma'am, but you certainly looked thirsty. I
   thought you wanted more.
Woman: But—
Waiter: And you must admit, you did let me *start* to pour.

I also heard the theory that awkwardness may occur because "rape introduces sex into the conversation." I found this observation useful because it's such a contrast to my view of a conversation about rape. I'm more likely to think I'm introducing *distress*. Or guilt.

Perhaps a comparison to the subject of death is most apt. Death immediately changes the stakes of a conversation to include the spiritual and the threatening. But for men, a conversation about rape can also include a fear of being held responsible and an embarrassing lack of familiarity with the subject. Most of us can manage a moment with a grieving person, can call to mind a word of comfort or an open-ended question to facilitate the exchange of feelings. But rape is *unspeakable*. We don't know how to smooth the path for the survivor or illuminate the darkness for the good of us all.

Once on an airplane I succumbed to the questions of a kind man who had noticed me writing. When I told him the subject of the manuscript, he took a long breath and disappeared into memory. "I knew a woman who felt she couldn't tell any of us what had happened. This was in college. She jumped off a bridge," he said, looking at me for an answer in the intimate darkness of the airplane, his sadness as visible as if he'd lost her yesterday.

A friend's son, after a frank discussion with his mother about his sexual behavior, said, "I never talked about it with you because I didn't want you to be disappointed in me." What's disappointing *to me* is that men and women have a problem to solve, and the lack of rhetorical ground rules may keep us from going after it.

B<small>EFORE WE HUNG UP</small> the phone that afternoon, Jim offered to investigate the availability of an apartment in the back of a house belonging to the parents of a friend. That phone call led us to St. Paul and the smallest apartment I'd ever seen. We stored our furnishings in various garages, having decided that we would look for a house rather than rent again. We moved in with a few clothes, a few dishes, and, illegally, our cat.

It was exactly right, as is often the case when we take our cues from the drift of universal forces. The tiny porch was all windows and just big enough for a couch and a television. Behind the porch was a passageway of a kitchen where I heated bowl after bowl of mushroom soup, which I ate while curled under a blanket watching television with the same indiscriminate intensity I had previously given to the plants. A bedroom and small bath completed the space; the total effect was of a hideaway, a place to go on from.

We had landed in St. Paul, the city across the river, whose shadings and noises were as foreign to me as if I'd crossed the continent. St. Paul friends introduced us to its charms during the weeks we lived there: the cathedral angels, the golden horses of the capitol, the backstreets of Crocus Hill with their lantern lights and lilacs. We didn't have a phone for a while, and I'd run to the pay phone on Grand Avenue, feeling as if I was rootless in the world, making calls with a pocketful of quarters, devising ways not to need a call in return. We watched summer turn to fall and the darkness come early enough to terrify. It was in that little apartment that the fear began. I'm glad those difficult nights were spent in a place we eventually left behind. I'm glad the first bouts with fear happened in a space so small that I could see *everything* from *anywhere*.

OVER LABOR DAY, Tim and I fled four hours north to a cabin on Lake Superior that we'd arranged to rent some months earlier. On the drive, we were subdued. I sunk into sadness, absorbed by the music filling the car, a tape Tim had made of our favorites. "Here Comes the Sun," the Beatles were insisting when I realized that we were pulling over to the side of the road. I looked up to see tears streaming down Tim's face. He appeared completely overcome, unable to drive in face of the lyrics we so loved.

I had cried only once up to this point and had seen no tears from Tim. I knew tears were a sign of emerging from shock, but I saw something else in Tim's racking sobs that I tried to ignore. I saw disappointment, what looked like despair, tears for the end of our long, sunny day. We'd been happy and lucky; we knew it. His eyes said he feared those days were over. What had happened to us confirmed something he'd always known or expected: life might offer to be good, but it won't last, and once it's gone, it's gone. He was not entirely right, but he was not entirely wrong. We chose up sides on exactly this issue, clinging stubbornly to our ideas about life's dynamics, insisting that the other see it our way. *Oh, to do some things over, to do them with vision this time.*

Our trip to Lake Superior gave us something to go on. We held each other in the cool, piney air and lay still to hear the birch leaves shudder. We found a rock where we could feel overwhelmed by stars. We made fires, drank scotch, lolled, took out a canoe. We had, in the words of Thomas Barry, "a moment of reconciliation with the divine." For the first time, I experienced what the heartsick have always known: the cold neutrality of the wild can help repair the breach. The lulling comfort of waves slapping on rocks is as available to the lost as the lucky. All that we loved had not deserted us, and we had not lost each other. We'd been knocked off our center, and we knew we had some distance to go. Yet if wisdom itself had taken me by the shoulders that weekend and said, *Listen, here's what you're in for,* I would have scoffed. I would not have believed any of what came next.

8

BEDTIME STORY / 2

"THE SNOW QUEEN"

THE SECOND PART

A LITTLE BOY AND A LITTLE GIRL

In the big city where there are so many houses and people that there is not enough room for everyone to have a little garden, and where, therefore, most people must content themselves with flowers in pots, there were two poor children who had a garden that was a little bigger than a flowerpot. They were not brother and sister but they were just as fond of one another as if they had been.

"Like me and Sofi," Andre interrupts.

"Best of friends," I say, brushing his hair from his eyes. Andre and Sofi stumbled around together as toddlers. Recently, they've sworn to marry. Years from this day, when Andre is in fifth grade, he'll portray their meeting on a banner he's asked to make depicting the Most Significant Events of His Life. He'll include no pictures of loss, no homage to his mother or father. He'll honor his guinea pigs, his friend Sofi, and learning how to read.

Kay and Gerda play under the rose trees on the rooftop all summer long, but winter keeps them apart. One day as they gaze at a picture book, Kay feels something pricking his heart and his eye.

After that, whenever Gerda came with the picture book, he said it was only fit for babies, and if grandmother told her tales, he was always ready to criticize. . . . It was the glass that he had got in his eye, the glass that had pierced his heart, and that was why he teased even little Gerda, who loved him with all her soul.

"Do you remember where the glass came from? We read that part a long time ago."

"That's for sure."

"You hardly fit under my arm anymore." Andre started school this year. His hair has gone tawny like his father's, but his eyes are still the color of Lake Superior ice—a blue encoded with summer. He'll grow up while I write this book and tell this story.

That winter, a great sled carrying a figure muffled in white comes to the town square. Kay decides to tie his toboggan to the back of the sled, and soon he is aloft, flying behind the Snow Queen high over the city. Though he shouts for help, no one can hear.

He was completely terrified and wanted to say the Lord's Prayer, but all he could remember were his multiplication tables.

They flew over forests and lakes, over land and sea, while below them the cold blast shrieked, the wolves howled, the snow sparkled, and over it flew the black screeching crows.

"What do you think?" I ask, closing the book. "Do you think he is in danger?"

Andre's eyes look at the same time innocent and fierce with understanding. "Of course!"

THE THIRD PART

THE FLOWER-GARDEN THAT BELONGED TO
THE OLD WOMAN WHO UNDERSTOOD MAGIC

But what happened to little Gerda when Kay came back no more? Where could he be? No one knew, no one had any news of him. . . .

Kay is dead and gone! said little Gerda.
I don't believe it! said the sunshine.
He's dead and gone! she said to the swallows.
I don't believe it! they answered, and at last little Gerda did
not believe it either.

Thinking Kay has fallen in the river, Gerda offers her most precious possession—a pair of red shoes—if the river will return the boy. But the river spits the shoes back.

Andre is busy laughing. It's the word *spit*. We've entered the stage where anything about the body is suspect and funny. Daily conversation is a minefield of double entendre. His guinea pigs squeak in their cages. We've inherited another one from Sofi's family, but she had to be renamed. Sweet Pea was unforgivably hilarious.

Gerda gets into a boat to throw the red shoes farther into the river. The boat shakes loose and takes Gerda downstream to a strange cottage with red and blue windows. A magical old woman with a spectacular garden rescues her and listens to her story.

I've been longing for a dear little girl like you, the old woman
said. With that, she buries the rosebushes in her garden so as not to remind Gerda of her other life. Eventually Gerda does remember the boy, and her tears fall to the ground, reviving the buried beauty of the roses.

Oh, what a lot of time I've wasted! said the little girl. Do you
think he's dead and gone?

No, he's not dead, said the roses. We've been in the earth where
all the dead are, but Kay wasn't there!

Gerda asks all the flowers in the garden if they know where Kay might be, and each flower in turn—the tiger-lily, the convolvulus, the snow-drop, the hyacinths, the buttercup, and the narcissus—tells a story, none of which concern Kay or help Gerda in any way. *It's no use talking to the flowers; they know*
only their own songs. Gerda runs out of the garden in frustration and sees that time is passing; it is autumn.

Oh, how grey and heavy it was in the wide world!

9

FEAR

Could you tell cottonwood
leaves in the cup from tea?
Is the moon in the tree
where the sun was,
and the wind in the leaves
like someone on the porch?

—LAURA JENSEN, "Dull Winter"

FEAR VISITED ME first in dreams that began, classically, as soon as I was in a place I felt safe, the cabin on Lake Superior. *I dreamt of it all for the first time last night, of a large, dark shape peering in at me from behind a door. I was frightened, but I knew it was a dream, and I could open my eyes.* What a lovely dream, I think now, in light of the detailed nightmares that were to come. I sense my own psyche just testing the waters—a single image thrown out to get the ball rolling, accompanied by immediate reassurance that this was a *dream*.

The experience of fear as a force in waking life did not begin until we'd settled into the little apartment in St. Paul. While the memory of the six weeks we lived there is coated with tenderness, it was, in fact, an introduction to a challenging and terrifying new reality.

Here's what the nights were like: *Felt the fear last night. Heard a floor creak and lost control. Like dominoes falling, the fear escalated. I had no thoughts, was not picturing or imagining, just feeling the panic, throat closing, shallow breaths, crying out, gripping Tim's arm, closing my eyes against it. Turning on the light and talking helped, though I lay awake a long time afterward. I'm glad that it happened. It wasn't unbearable, though it would have been harder if I'd been alone.*

And this entry from two weeks later: *It comes every other night, lasting from 4:30 to 5:30 A.M., but expressed without words or thoughts, simply through my body. Waking to a floor squeak and finding myself fully in the grip of panic, small yelps, like those of a wounded animal, taking the place of the silence I forced myself into that night. I'm reliving it again and again, but this time experiencing the full terror of it. It occurs to me that one reason I have not been writing much here is that words seem unimportant in this period of pure feeling.*

My sister, who saved her own life by jumping out the window of a burning house, knows the body's insistence that reenactments occur in real time. She woke, in a house on fire, to what she thought was the sound of rain. For many months afterward, she could not sleep a moment past five-thirty; each night was broken according to schedule, almost as if a part of the soul, having become separated from the body, tried night after night to regain entry just at the moment it was lost.

It begins right after we go to bed, or intrudes upon the midnight hours, always the early mornings. I get up and run a bath, hoping the change of activity will distract me from my unswerving belief in disaster. But as I soak beneath the comforting yellow light, I worry that when I splash the water, Tim will rustle the sheets as he turns over in bed, and we will miss the critical moment, the moment danger has chosen to slip a key in the door. I learn to sit perfectly still, to ignore the sound of my heart pounding, my blood blurting along through my body, the *thrum* of the furnace, the rasp of the refrigerator. I hear beyond these masking noises. I note every sound, examine it, wait to see if it amplifies into disaster, breathe, wait for the next one.

We sleep in a room fully lit. *My nights are broken, yellow light staring in our eyes.* I wear a nightgown. I wear my glasses. I keep a can of tear gas by my side. I wake Tim at all hours. In the morning, we get up and go to work. And when people ask, I say that I am fine.

OCTOBER and the trees along Summit Avenue turn bittersweet. The dark comes hard and fast. Many nights I do not make it to our lighted windows before the fear does. I find that I cannot get out of the car and walk up the short driveway to the front door in the early dark. *It's a burning, a singe of alertness like a finger abruptly run down the spine.*

The neighborhood in which I find myself paralyzed is old St. Paul genteel. It brings to mind England. Called Crocus Hill, it draws its sense of style from the grace of the homes a few blocks away on the broad boulevard of Summit Avenue, the street where F. Scott Fitzgerald fled into the snowy night, banging on cars after his first novel was accepted for publication. Though bordered by less placid sections, anyone would pronounce the neighborhood dull.

Not me. Once the impossible has occurred, possibility becomes its most compelling feature. Animals still, we recategorize immediately when death lunges from behind the tree where we're accustomed to suckling our young. The human being in fear has been tipped off to something the idiots around her cannot see. She knows better, knows the folded darkness is crowded with possibilities. Trying to talk me out of this hypervigilance is as fruitless as arguing with a schizophrenic about identity. I live in an altered state whose reality has the authority of madness.

On nights I know I will not reach home before dark, I call to alert Tim. *The heart wears shoes, thuds its clumsy way into flight.* He meets me at the curb and escorts me up the driveway. We do this many times. I am only slightly embarrassed, and he seems to take it in stride. We both behave as if I need help managing crutches or some such conventional crippling. Looking back, I wince. *That afraid, that stricken,* my inner voice still whispers, a bit shamed and disbelieving. I marvel that I could have spent several hours facing down the possibility of actual death and, as a consequence, be paralyzed by a quiet driveway.

My friend Jim said, *You may have to feel it in your body before you can stop turning it over in your mind,* and I wrote that down. I *appeared* to be paying attention to the role my body was playing in these fearful reenactments, but in truth, I did not understand how completely my body was in charge. It was not until the next time I experienced physical trauma—during labor—that I recognized the existence of bodily memory.

On both occasions, I noticed a curious feeling of sympathy for my body, as if the mind/body split were actual, and I could send a reassuring note to the poor thing. *Last night I felt hurt, actual pain. I sat in bed crying ouch, ouch, ouch, ouch, thought about how my body has had a hard year, cried for the harm to cease.*

One might understandably medicate oneself through this period, though for me it lasted long enough to make that option dangerous. What is not clear to me is whether the physiological reactions diminished of their own accord, or if these nights on the edge of death from which I consistently woke unharmed retrained me to a more normal reaction pattern. In other words, did I have to live through terror in order to reach the diminishment of its symptoms?

I believe that my sense of tenderness toward the apartment on Linwood, the endless bowls of mushroom soup, the tension in the autumn dark, stems from this need to know, to experience again and again in my body and my imagination a new possibility. The demands of normal life were missing, and I operated under the waivers granted the invalid. I spent the dark nights curled up on the couch, watching television gratefully and uncritically, Tim holding me on the evenings he was home as we prepared for the hard work of the night.

M Y COUNSELOR at the Rape and Sexual Assault Center puts it gently, as if she knows I will not understand it. *You have to build an extra room onto your house for the fear.* We're sitting in the plain second-floor room of the house where the center is located, uncomfortable on the mismatched donated chairs. *Crisis counseling lasts six weeks,* Dorothy explains during our first session that September. *After that, we recommend a support group for ten weeks. Then you'll have the tools to really begin dealing with the issues.*

She cautions me not to expect real change for six months, to look at three years of serious work toward the vague goal of recovery, something she calls "integration." I'm listening hard, wanting to do it right. But I can't believe what I'm hearing. I laugh. *Three years! I don't have three weeks to give this. I don't intend this to take up any more of my time than it already has,* I say, as if I've got the power to negotiate on this.

Wasn't she a saint not to laugh right back at me? She knew what I know now. It would be closer to ten years before I had "dealt with the issues." My outburst seems to me now an acknowledgment of the change that was blooming in me, taking hold like a cell dividing, gathering energy for the next growth even as the first division was occurring, spinning an organism of unknown dimension out of itself, unstoppable. I wanted it stopped. I was unwilling to feed it. I was inclined to turn my back on my own evolution, reluctant to take charge of a process I believed did not belong to me. I was a long way from "integration."

Instead I coped. Get over it and get on with it, I told myself. I inherited this notion from my father, for whom virtue is measured in hard work. Mewling about gets in the way of hard work. I added my own spice to the mix, bringing in pride and a determination made of innate stubbornness and feminist conditioning.

In November, when I do finally tell my father what has happened, he offers predictable advice. *You've got to put it behind you*, he says, his attention focused on his shoe. I look away myself in that moment, picturing a wagon I cannot lose but that needs to be out of sight "behind me." *You can't let this get you down*, he advises. His intentions are good. He has raised his four children to be tenacious survivors, but I already *am* down. What am I to do now? I need a way to proceed that takes *trauma* into account.

But I don't have that language yet. I don't realize that my symptoms describe a condition about which there is knowledge, a condition I share with war veterans, plane crash survivors, and battered women. A condition I share with my father. After years of war stories about lively hijinks on the open sea, my father recently revealed that he has dreamed about World War II nearly every night since his return. Judith Herman describes the condition we now know as post-traumatic stress this way.

> *Traumatic reactions occur when action is of no avail. When neither resistance nor escape is possible, the human system of self-defense becomes overwhelmed and disorganized. Each component of the ordinary response to danger, having lost its utility, tends to persist in an altered and exaggerated state long after the actual danger is over. Traumatic events produce profound and lasting changes in physiological arousal, emotion, cognition, and memory.*

After a traumatic experience, the human system of self-preservation seems to go on permanent alert, as if danger might return at any moment.

This made startling reading for me when I encountered it in *Trauma and Recovery* in 1992. Called "one of the most important psychiatric works to be published since Freud," Herman's book gave me immediate relief, a perspective on symptoms whose persistence had seemed a personal failure. Why couldn't I get over this? Why, when it was happening, couldn't I talk myself out of it? I knew I was "safe," but fear had all the momentum.

"Victims of a devastating trauma may never be the same biologically," according to Dr. Dennis Charney, director of clinical neuroscience at the National Center for Post-Traumatic Stress Disorder in an interview in the *New York Times*. His research focuses on three locations in the brain involved in mobilizing the body for an emergency. All three, recent research indicates, are permanently altered by trauma.

Two of the sites regulate hormones: the adrenaline and noradrenaline that put our bodies on alert, and CRF, the stress hormone released to kick off the flight-or-fight response. The third site secretes endorphins, which dull pain and, when overstimulated, may account for the emotional numbness that is perhaps the biggest heartbreak of life after rape. *Feeling is gone,* I wrote, and to this day, I paw at the batting that muffles the roaring of my old heart. Who would I be if I still had that fertile, silty river flowing through me? This is always the question as we age, but there's a sense of being robbed of *a way of being* following trauma, which may be accounted for by the brain's response to overwhelming terror.

Under extreme stress, it appears, our mechanisms for self-preservation become overstimulated. After the danger has passed, they do not revert to normal. The exaggerated reactivity persists, as if a switch has been thrown so hard it has become stuck. And when the mechanism has been damaged, when it rings and rings and rings, the fear itself begins to terrorize. "The patient is, one might say, fixated to the trauma. This astonishes us far too little," observed Sigmund Freud in a time when the crippling symptoms of post-traumatic stress were dismissed as "shell shock" or "hysteria."

Descriptions of these symptoms by trauma survivors are highly consistent: "a feeling of intense fear, helplessness, loss of control, and threat of annihilation," catalogs the *Comprehensive Textbook of Psychiatry.* Testimonies at a serial rape trial are summarized this way in a newspaper account: "They talked of how their lives had changed in fundamental ways because of the rapes. They talked of such things as jobs lost, of sleepless nights, of relationships ended, of moving out of places that had once been home."

Yet whenever I read such descriptions, I notice a curious glazing over in my heart. The words themselves are clear enough, but I've seen these symptoms somewhere before—in a TV movie perhaps, and as a result, I sense they don't last more than a few minutes of screen time. Curiously, the truth about what it means to survive rape—that you are literally changed—is obscured by the predictability of the symptoms used to convey it.

Love is a word with no love in it, I tell my writing students, quoting the poet Donald Hall. Avoid abstractions, I say. Show us the peculiar way love looks to you, and we will learn something useful about loving. Later in the same newspaper account, a detail appears that expresses what I know to be true about fear. "She said that because her assault occurred in the fall, the sound of leaves makes her afraid."

A CAT IN THE UNDERBRUSH, complete darkness, an obstructed view, reading in bed, voices through an open window, summer rain. My relationship to fear looks something like the way skiers handle the occasional moose that turns up on the slopes outside Anchorage. *You wait for the moose to move,* my friends Gwen and Melissa tell me. Sometimes, you have to spend an hour standing perfectly still in the cold when you'd rather be flying through the air or drinking hot chocolate. *You don't try to go around a moose in the path.* At less than half my age, they understand something that feminism couldn't teach me about fear.

Submission, in a word. Not a comfortable notion when its object is fear, when its subject is a woman who has been raped. But animals know this strategy, choose watchfulness early in an encounter with a new threat while they gather their forces for attack or defense. *You must build an extra room on your house for the fear.* Had I been able to heed this advice, I might have been spared a year of darkness. As it was, I resisted, believing I could overpower my reality with my will, my pride, my capacity for suffering.

THE DIFFICULT NIGHTS continued past the brutal but protected weeks in St. Paul and accompanied us to our new house in Minneapolis. It was the worst possible time to buy a house. Anyone could have told us that, and many people did. Interest rates were 17 percent. Winter was coming. Our lawyer, the father of a friend pressed into service at the last moment, met us for dinner on the way to a concert with his wife, mumbling: *This is no way to buy a house.*

To make things worse, an odd notion of entitlement made me certain that the perfect house was not only available but our *due.* We'd had a bad break, and now the universe would set it straight. But our Realtor hadn't gotten the word, and she kept showing us houses that had no light, no room for an office, bad paneling, cramped rooms, narrow hallways, noisy streets. There was no end to what I did not like. Despite sleep deprivation, we looked at every house on the market in our price range and found nothing.

Then, as if the universe really did climb on the bandwagon, we took a Sunday drive in the neighborhood we longed for and came upon a house with a sign FOR SALE BY OWNER. It took us until the first of November to move in, but the deal was struck in my heart when I saw the corner lot and the sunporches, the modest but well-tended yard, and the bolt locks on the doors front and back. The owners turned it over to us with an endearing reluctance and ceremony, as if entrusting a beloved to our care. I've remained in touch with them, but I've never asked if they could see in our faces how wounded we were and in need of shelter.

We moved in a few weeks before my thirtieth birthday. By this time, I had completed crisis counseling and was slated to join a support group. I came to hate the group almost as much as I'd learned to love my sessions with Dorothy. The other women were at least a year into their recovery, and they were in distressing shape.

Confidentiality means not going into detail here, and in truth my difficulties with the group had little to do with the other women. I didn't want to be there, waste time, know how much there was to deal with down the line, listen to other people's troubles. I wanted to be okay, happy about our house. I wanted to "put it behind me." Instead, every Saturday I sat in the living room of the center with nine other women in various states of disarray and refused to be helped.

Our FIRST MEETING was the Saturday morning of moving day, warm as June with October's colors slicing across the sky. A day when the world cannot be faulted. Yet, when I return from the session and find myself alone in the empty house, I see the dominion of the inner landscape. Tim is loading a truck somewhere, and as soon as I enter the house, the panic begins. It gets its way with me very quickly.

Unlike the tiny apartment, where every room was visible

from every other room, this house has three floors, innumerable hiding spaces, and seems to undulate with emergency. I tiptoe through the empty spaces across the shining hardwood floors, the sunlight a distant call from someone else's life. Peering into closets and behind doors, my anxiety grows, the pressure in my chest and in my legs builds until I bolt down the stairs, rush to the front porch, slam the door, crazed by the knowledge that I've outrun only the visible threats. I'm still vulnerable to the surprise attack, to whatever I cannot see. Crouching low beneath the porch windows, I lock both doors, lock myself both in and out.

I pass the time in the state known as "hypervigilance," listening, scanning, adrenaline pumping up my breath, poised literally on my toes for an invisible and therefore tricky, tricky opponent. I emerge as exhausted by the effort as if I'd truly had a brush with danger. This is one of the aspects of post-traumatic fear that is hardest to convey. Imagine how tired you'd be if you defended your house from intruders every night for a month or survived a car crash each night for a year.

It is in recalling this incident that I retrieve the sensation of craziness that post-traumatic fear can provoke. I got a partial answer to my childhood musings about what it would be like to be crazy. It would be terrible, at least in this stage, when my allegiance remained with reason, but I was unable to operate reasonably. When suddenly one's actions are dictated by imagination and by projections clearly not based in rational thought, then one worries even as one obeys.

I'm still frozen on the porch when Tim arrives. He looks puzzled and a bit discouraged as he realizes what has happened. His spirits are up. We are finally moving on. He is desperate for this move to signal the end of my difficulties, the resumption of our life together. He does not tell me so. He does what he did so many times that first year: holds me, talks me through it, leads me inside, urging me toward a decision about where the couch should go. We both feel the blow;

we've been hoping to leave our demons in St. Paul. Instead, the fear will not be ignored. Its territory will expand like the circles of a stone dropped in water. Fear will follow me whenever I travel away from it, insistent and ingenious.

IT FOLLOWS ME to Arizona that winter where our friends Beth and Jack arrange writing work for me so we can afford a respite bathed in the ministry of Beth's laughter. The nightmares come too, rousting us in the middle of the night to the dying echo of full-throated screams—was that me?—then the embarrassment: Have I woken the people in the next room? I remember a morning in Florida nearly two years later. The memory of my screams drew stares from our fellow vacationers as I emerged from the flimsy cabins on the beach the next morning. I imagined some of them were surprised to see me alive. In others, curiosity seemed to battle with irritation: Isn't there some kind of law?

In April, after successfully ignoring Tim's suggestion that I enter individual therapy, I ram my car into the back of a van at a stoplight. As the driver and I lie in the emergency room to have our minor injuries treated, I realize that I had not been *in* the car, not that afternoon nor for a very long time. Instead of living my actual life—afraid, angry, wounded—I am living elsewhere, skimming the surface enough to appear to function but capable of checking out so completely I forget I am driving a car. A few weeks later, I begin therapy.

DONNA IS A QUIET, bespectacled woman, younger than I, and she introduces me to therapy in its conventional sense. My journal from this period is full of the standard revelations about arrested development, my skewed view of my parents, notes on codependency and family systems. I love this stuff. It's concrete. You can take notes on it, possibly master it, and use it to control your future, maybe even your past. But Donna's position on fear is less engaging. Simply put: It will never go away. And don't think you're the only woman who feels it.

Never go away? What's the point of talking to you if you aren't going to make the fear go away? I like Donna, like thinking about my childhood, but my life has become the servant of my fear, and it's her job to make that stop. She meets my objections with a calm refusal to insist on her viewpoint, and a calm refusal to alter it. I ignore Donna's position on fear and fill my notebook with deconstructions of family mythologies. Yet scattered throughout the eager-beaver notations are the nightmares, two and three a week, week after week, through the rest of that first year.

I was alone in a big house and couldn't keep all the doors and windows shut, had to keep closing them. My cat and I wanted to go for a walk in the rain, but I felt we shouldn't without locking everything up. We walked briefly, and when we came back, I heard a kid trying to break in upstairs.

I went up and yelled at him, then explained that I was a nice person—I was a teacher, and students liked me. He and his friends left. As soon as I closed the windows, I realized there was someone in the house. I jumped out onto the roof, waited, and saw a man with long black hair come out onto the roof. I jumped down to the sidewalk and ran but couldn't scream. Then the dream switched, and I was dreaming and screaming so loud I'd bitten my lip, and I was bleeding and Tim couldn't hear me.

For a full year, it's as if demons were called forth every night to wrestle for my allegiance—clever, inventive, relentlessly performing. I have not had a nightmare in a decade. I eventually exhausted the possibilities for terror, it seems, and was left with the blessing of undisturbed sleep.

• • •

Before I was raped, I had reluctantly taken a self-defense class at the urging of a friend. This same friend had convinced me to take tap dancing with her earlier, a fairly embarrassing little experiment that should have convinced her of what I already knew, *This is not my area.* But off I went, persuaded that I should learn how to defend myself but doubtful whether one class would give me such confidence. The course was taught by a woman whose main goal became to get me to stop smiling when I delivered a body blow. She said I wouldn't progress until I got furious. I remember feeling only a little silly, mustering up imaginary moxie to practice what felt like another arcane series of dance steps I couldn't quite remember week to week.

Rape forces you to take stock of your vulnerability. But to take action requires harnessing your fear to your anger. Olympic swimmer Nancy Hogshead talks of beginning to train seriously after surviving rape. A clear-eyed young woman I know turned almost instinctively to weight lifting to restore her confidence and her courage. But I turned away. The blow to the spirit that I took on the chin that night knocked me flat, and in that weakened state I had no access to that kind of hope.

When spring arrives and I set out for walks around the city lakes, the fear moves out of the house and begins to claim the world of daylight and open spaces.

Lake Harriet, one of four lakes in a cluster near downtown Minneapolis, lies an easy walk from my house and startles me still with its loveliness, its chameleon heart. Three miles around and swimmable, it can look like an ocean bay when the halyards of the sailboats are clanging, like a Swedish village when the neighborhood gathers at the blue pavilion for summer music, or it can hold the isolation of a remote northern lake on a Wednesday morning in early spring when few walkers cross one's path and the sloping hillsides become hiding places.

As I swing out my door and make my thoughtless way to the lake, I watch placid mornings become exhausting exercises. Each moment presents danger before me, danger behind me, danger—around that curve, behind that bush, in that parked car, anywhere, anywhere. How rapidly one can calculate the exponents of disaster. Stride, stride—a clump of bushes—stride, stride—a clump of bushes near a curve in the path—*threat squared*. Add early-morning solitude, the sound of a car radio, the way the path veers below the sloping hillside, the fact that no one ever seems to be home in these big old houses, and you raise the equation to an incalculable power.

Then it begins: the steel-trap throat, the rocketing heartbeat, the world's goodness transparent as rice paper. Finally, the meditative walks I love become impossible. At home, the walls quiver, but if I stay alert, never take a shower when alone, never answer the door without my tear gas (even to the startled meter reader, more frightened than I), I can survive a sunny day in the safest neighborhood in Minneapolis.

One of the women in my therapy group related her strategy for managing a walk around the lake. She carried a raw egg in each pocket, kept one in her hand, a ready missile should she be surprised by anything. Up to that point, she had not needed her eggs for defensive purposes, but she never wasted them. She'd fire them at trees, practicing her delivery, cursing the air around her as she ate up the ground, her short legs pounding the blacktop, her jaw set, her close-cropped hair exposing a young and troubled face, steeled against the daylight, courageous in her acceptance of her own fear and her resourceful strategies for living with it. I'd listened to her then with slight horror and in disbelief, but I have since felt only admiration for her refusal to stop walking.

• • •

JUDE, my closest friend from college, comes to see how I am doing. Deeply afraid of flying, she travels by train from Ann Arbor, displaying the strenuous loyalty of an easterner making her way west by wagon train after a friend's letters have stopped arriving. In her company I see how fear has overrun my life.

On a muggy weekday afternoon late in her visit, we set out to walk to Lake Harriet. A summer storm hangs over the lake, and just as we reach a hillside park overlooking the water, the rain begins. A picnic shelter under a vaulted roof open on all sides is a dry and reasonably comfortable place to wait out the cloudburst. We enter, laughing with that reckless ecstasy that endures from childhood, but within a minute, I turn silent. We have been joined in the huge open space by a stranger. He appears without our noticing, suddenly there, hanging out on the opposite side of the round shelter.

As I attempt, in writing this, to reenter the emotional confusion that caused me to react as I did to his presence, I am stopped. The woman I was, so afraid of a man I am now certain was perfectly ordinary, is a vanished self. I can see her from a distance, can follow her movements and guess with a storyteller's accuracy how she misread the situation, but *reporting* her state of mind is blessedly beyond me now, an odd signpost of the distance I've traveled.

SHE STOPS TALKING. *She watches him. He rocks back and forth on his heels, looks out toward the lake, then right at her and away again. His eyes are hooded, his body lean. He has no age, no reason to be here. Why is he here? He crosses to a different picnic table, slightly closer to them. Why doesn't he leave? Anything could happen, so everything starts beating—a heart that can outrun a bear, ears turned inward to catch jumbled and impossible warnings, eyes to see just slightly into the future, into the next moment when the man will cross over to them, pull a knife, shoot, speak.*

Let's go, she insists. Her friend looks stupidly unaware of any danger, gazing off toward a seagull circling.

Go? Her friend gestures to the downpour, sheets of rain now, the plashing, pounding height of the storm. Her friend laughs, actually turns away, as if this conversation is casual.

We can't stay here, the woman hisses, gesturing with her head toward the man who is definitely watching them, definitely listening. The look on her friend's face is memorable, as if some devastating news has just registered. The woman interprets this as agreement and only later realizes that her friend was devastated by her, by the realization that fear had escalated to paranoia and is about to drive them out into the pouring rain.

They bolt out of the shelter, slipping on the wet grass, scaling the hill, running, running, until, dripping wet, they reach the safety of commerce, the neighborhood stores a block away. Later as they walk home, she tells her friend that something important has happened. She has never been this far into the territory that shadows her. She did not know she could go this far. And more importantly, this is the end. She cannot live this way anymore.

AFTER THE INCIDENT in the rain, I relent. It is a quiet act, nearly invisible, a decision of the spirit. I begin to take the advice I've been given, and it works. As soon as I treat fear with deference, fear retreats. I begin to build the room Dorothy had envisioned for me, the room Donna urged me toward, the room I resent. I learn to take immediate action. I learn to say *I'm afraid*. Sometimes the sound of a human voice is enough to bridge the moment. If it is very late, I call the time or weather.

We install a bolt lock on our bedroom door, a tip from a friend whose husband travels extensively. The genius of this idea lies in its simplicity, its low-tech implementation, and the decisive sound of the bolt sliding into place. I buy several canisters of tear gas (legal in Minnesota only since 1981), which I never expect to use but that provide the comfort of a nonlethal weapon.

Yet there are nights when the fear asserts itself beyond the logic of a bolt lock. *What about the second-floor window; someone might have entered the house earlier in the day; a really strong person could break down the door.* For these times I need excess. I develop a routine that presumes there is an actual threat to my life in progress: bolt lock on, lights on, glasses on, tear gas in hand, remote phone nearby, perfect attention for the slightest noise, *be still, still, is it a rustling, the intake of breath?* I go through the motions, and fully armed against a placid night, I can settle into sleep.

Eventually I arrive at an image that continues to shore me up. I see myself rising out of my bed in a powerful dancer's leap, meeting the rapist in midair before he has a chance to come crashing down on my sleeping form. I place my hand flat on his chest and push him, still floating in air, down the hallway and out onto the front porch, where three men from my life materialize. They surround him—powerful, unswerving, united—and stand guard while I glide out the front door.

In another time, Virginia Woolf prescribed a room of one's own as a necessary component for the liberation of a woman's mind. It is with no small sadness that I endorse the prescription of a room for one's fear for the women of my time. It is a prescription that has caused rebellion in the generation of women who follow me, and I am heartened by that spirit. Yet simply to assert women's strength fails to account for the truth. There is a moose on the path, and when walking there we are wise to acknowledge its presence. Denying danger empowers danger.

Similarly, I have noticed a tendency for women to dismiss the experience of an attempted rape as minor, assigning it to an entirely different category than the assault that includes sexual penetration. Women have described to me "close calls" from which an enduring fear response was triggered though no rape or assault took place. While rape provokes its own constellation of difficulties, one of the most profound—traumatic fear—has its grip on great numbers of women who mistakenly believe their experience unworthy of attention. Their bouts with fear become a private shame, a personal failing. Not taken seriously, fear always becomes serious. Dying counts, fear of dying counts, and even momentary terror endures in the traumatized memory until we give it room.

How I Walk

I walk with my keys inserted
    between each space
in my hand. I use only two
    keys in my real life
but keep two from some past lives
    I've led so I can have
all four spaces filled.

    I lace my keys between my fingers
        of my left hand, my power
    hand, the hand strong from writing,
        the hand strong because it's
    connected to my strongest arm, strong
        left arm that's carried my babies.

So now I'm walking. Can you see me?
    I am a big woman, and I walk fast.
If you look closely you can see the glint
    of the tips of my keys. It's a flash,
not like a diamond. I don't have diamonds;
    it's four flashes: light   light
light   light. When I come home from walking
    my fist is cramped from keeping
the tips of my keys at attention.

I'm older now, have too many jobs,
        I don't walk four miles a day anymore.
When I walk now all I see are dogs
        connected to women by metal chains,
leather chains, so really I think of them
        as dog-chained-women, or maybe women-
chained-dogs. I no longer reach out
        my hand, palm up, to any dog,
the women have told me they do not want
        their dogs to make friends
with strangers. These women tied to dogs
        are all sizes. Some as tall as I am,
some taller, some have warrior faces,
        some cupid faces, some have lines
putting new faces on top of old faces,
        some are shockingly beautiful,
some are tiny.

Tiny women connected to dogs
        always made sense to me.
These tiny women are vulnerable,
        I thought, so many years
ago. I thought, tiny women must be
        frightened. I have always
had in my circle of women, tiny
        women friends. Tiny meaning:
perfect, to me, a big woman. One
        small friend of mine just
wrote a brilliant essay about walking
        in a woman's body; one dearest
small friend, raped years ago,
        no dog in the apartment
to take the knife in her place.

Whenever I walk with that friend
    I've always thought,
she is safe with me. I am big and walk
    with extraordinary purpose.
If someone came toward us with menace
    as we walked the circle of
the lake, I know I would kill that person,
    would hurl my key hand into
his eye, his delicate throat, and I would
    tell my friend to run to the
nearest tree and climb it and I would find
    her in the branches, my keys would
be bloody, my hand damaged but still full
    of power.

I walk with my keys and pretend
    they give me all I need.
I pretend because I have size I will
    always be safe. Some friends
of mine who are small have never
    been attacked. Some friends
of mine, my size, have been raped and beaten.
    If I think about this I might
stop walking. And I was not there
    to save my friend the night
she was cut and raped. I have not been able
    to save friends, children, strangers.

How I walk is with my keys, alone
    or with a friend, I walk
full of vengeance and denial, I walk
    in fear where once I walked
in poetry, in love, in the light
    of the blessed sun, the blessed moon.

—DEBORAH KEENAN

IO

FIRST ANNIVERSARY

August 14, 1982

For those whose vanished past is something to miss as much as to transcend, happiness looks back over its own shoulder, tugged by nostalgia for what has already been or will inevitably be lost. Yet what is gazed back at is also the fullness of what can never be taken away.

—RACHEL HADAS, *The Double Legacy*

THE FIRST ANNIVERSARY was full of foreboding and gratitude. Exactly at the six-month point, I'd had an elaborate encoded dream alerting me that my internal clock was keeping track. I wondered if this day and its night would entail reliving the experience with similar brilliance.

Tim and I decided to mark the anniversary with a picnic on our sunroom floor—the reason for making this choice escapes me now. As we sat together eating cheese and olives and chocolate, I remember feeling no happiness though we smiled at each other as if this were a party we wanted to attend. At some point, like an emblem of the year's ironic blessings, an extravagant bouquet of flowers and a pretty good bottle of champagne arrived. Attached was a note of congratulations from our friend Jim. The bitter tang of that mix of celebration and defeat has lessened as the years pass, but it still sharpens my tongue every August 14.

Mostly, I recall trying to thank Tim for all he had done and been that year. I remember choosing my words carefully, hoping my offering would be sufficient to the task. I was the thirsty one, and he had let me drink without limit. I knew his throat had grown painfully dry.

Fairy tales are full of stories about the burden of gratitude borne toward one who has saved your life. The stories detail the lengths the saved will go to acknowledge that debt, for the saved know the fragility of what was nearly lost. The saved know the critical moment in which life becomes death, know that grace and courage must intercede forcefully because the water rushing over the cliff has tremendous momentum. The saved know the value of the one who sees past good cheer, stops by once a day, offers a loan, blocks the blow. The saved know and can't express their gratitude adequately.

We are always saving one another. Sometimes we are aware of it; we notice the cost to our reserves even as we pay it. Other times we are unaware that we have grown wings, swooped someone from danger without ever glancing behind or feeling the weight of our temporary feathers. But the saved know, and so the stories accumulate. In the fairy tale "The Fisherman and His Wife" she asks for endless repayment, eventually commanding power over church and state because the faithful fish, spared once by the fisherman, cannot refuse her.

I have tried to detail Tim's steadfast interventions, but some acts can never be acknowledged adequately; they are gifts. It is these that stretch the hearts of the giver and the receiver, that call out for metaphor, for the stories and fables we read to our children as instruction. *You will be called upon to give beyond your means, to sacrifice for others who may never know it was your lifeblood that revived their own. In this way, we humans become great. In this way, we understand love.*

II

ROOTS OF FEAR

Some of the most interesting people I've ever met have been strangers. The Nepalese acknowledge strangers on the path with the greeting, "The god in me greets the god in you." But in my childhood, the stranger was the godless face of danger. Awash in warnings, I feared a cartoon man in a trench coat and porkpie hat who would jump out of a car or from behind the bushes at the fire station on Eleven Mile Road to give me candy.

Yet, my mother talked to strangers. Everywhere. On the bus, in shops, on Girl Scout field trips to the doll hospital or the Henry Ford Museum. A great deal of our daily conversation revolved around puzzling out the behavior or story of the strangers we'd encountered that day. "Isn't that an unusual suit," she'd say, and I'd nod automatically. "I'll bet he's got a couple of kids at home, and he's just trying to look his best." Or: "She's the kind of person you'd like to know your whole life long. Just like your Aunt Barbara—a rock."

She taught me to look for opportunities to exercise my curiosity. I have taught Andre to talk to strangers. Yet, when he rides off on his bicycle, when he's gone too long in a public rest room, I fear for his safety like any mother with information and imagination. The threat from strangers is nearly always associated with sexual predation. What I fear most is that something will happen about which he will never speak, a loss kept secret and allowed to shadow his joy, ravage his courage, poison his future without warning me of the need for an antidote.

COULD IT BE, Donna asked one day as we sat in her cubicle, the kind provided for therapists who treat patients on a sliding scale, *that you have always been afraid? No*, I thought, *not always*. In our born bodies, we are not afraid. Watch any girl child before harm has been done and you'll see the open-armed embrace, the rush toward sensation. Childhood prepared me to assume power and to defer to it. I was a dreamy girl with big plans. I formed a neighborhood club so that I could be president, wrote plays so that I could make my brother take the bit parts, sometimes requiring him to wear a blue pigtail wig.

My mother had majored in political science in college and remained fiercely interested in politics all her life. Her mother had a short career as a singer in New York before her marriage. I clung to this legacy of high ambitions, but I was made to practice the fine points of manners and learned how to iron pleats and polish silver. I bent to my father's temper, learned to assess his moods, kept my thoughts to myself.

I became a reader, Nancy Drew, the gothics of Phyllis Whitney, then straight to Camus. I took the voyage out toward a life of ideas, little black dresses, wind in my hair, toward the romance of adventure as much as the lure of a reckless embrace. Where was fear in all this? A hum in the soundtrack, a bee in the garden, a steady deposit of knowledge, from the innuendo of Sunday supplement cartoons to the desperate tears of the winners on *Queen for a Day*. I noticed Cary Grant decking Katharine Hepburn in my favorite movie, *Philadelphia Story*. I noted the glances that passed between my mother and her friends, the stories that slipped out before someone realized I was listening. *Little pitchers* . . . Mrs. Peters or my aunt

Eleanor would intone, and I'd be left with just a scrap of excitement to embroider later that night in the dark.

Stitched together they amounted to a flash of color at the back of consciousness, not enough to prevent me from taking chances, from having my way with my life. But looking back, I see the pattern, how it readied me to read the world for danger. *Don't think you're the only woman who is afraid*, said Donna. *Don't think you're the only woman.*

W HEN I ASK my mother to recall incidents that may have schooled me in female fear, she answers quickly, "I can't think of anything." I press her. She casts back into what seem like calm waters. I can see this question doesn't resonate with her sense of my childhood. Then, "Your father was on the road a lot when we lived on Eleven Mile." Her eyes drift, brighten. She is pulling a night out of the past, no longer responding to my question but to a memory she seems surprised to have retrieved.

"One summer night when I was home alone with you kids," she continues in her storytelling voice, "a young man rang the doorbell and asked if he could have some water for his radiator. His car had overheated, he said." There's hesitation in her delivery; she's reacquainting herself with this memory as she tells it. "I let him in," she says with finality. "I shouldn't have done that."

She is far away in a life I never really shared with her—her marriage and young motherhood. "After he left, Donald Elliot marched up to the door to bawl me out. He'd been watering his azaleas, and he'd seen the man on my porch. 'Don't ever do that again,' he said. 'Don't ever let a stranger into your house when Joe's not home.'"

As I listen, I am startled to realize that I, too, remember this night. The image I carry could easily have come from a dream or an episode of *Dragnet*, but as my mother talks, I recognize it as an emotional memory, the quality of the moment transferred to me. The cicadas, the summer dark, a man on the sidewalk in a white undershirt—Mr. Elliot. A strange car hunched in the driveway, the stranger—his oily, wavy hair, his tight pants nothing like the dacron trousers worn by the neighborhood fathers. I remember fastening on him through the soft mesh of the screen door, but mostly my memory is made of what I can only describe as an aurora of intensity around the scene and its players, fear making indelible an otherwise unremarkable fifteen minutes from my childhood.

I DIDN'T LOOK in the casket, in the basement of Our Lady of LaSallette that rainy November morning, stiff flowers closing the boy off from view. Petey Peters lived two doors down from us in the brown house with the depressing marigolds edging the lawn. His father was a librarian, his mother, a coffee drinker with dark circles under her eyes who showed up at our house during thunderstorms to sit on a lawn chair in the basement with my mother, who was, herself, not at all afraid of thunder. I can hardly remember Petey's face without the puffy, leukemia cheeks, the hard brown eyes sunk into his face like raisins on a cookie.

He grew enormous before he died round and quiet. We never played Superman in the backyard or crab attack in the basement after he got sick, sick from that word I practiced saying so that I would know it. Petey Peters got *leukemia* and died a quiet, faintly smiling seven-year-old death, and I couldn't look at him in his casket. I wanted to, but I couldn't move from my spot at the rear of the crowded room.

The colors had all yellowed in the church basement light, the flowers heavy as clubs, the black backs of women in wool suits and veils, and Mr. and Mrs. Peters leaning into each other as if they had lost their spines. I could not look, not even when my mother, supposing I needed to grieve head-on, took my hand and helped me walk toward the casket, not when the music played and my mysteriously brave sister, who was his true best friend, marched right up to lay a rose on his casket. Not ever.

Now that I have a son, I think of Petey's death differently. Then it seemed frightening and mysterious but in line, somehow, with everything else that happened. I did not find the Peters family particularly tragic or in need of my admiration, as I certainly do now. They later adopted a boy of the same age, and Stevie Peters became our friend on the block.

But something did frighten me deeply in that church, something I can still locate when I call the scene to mind, some truth escaped my defense system and froze a part of me in place, wanting and needing to see my dead friend but unable to move toward him. Wanting and needing to remain unmoved by death but unable to deny it.

I LEARNED THE WORD *sniper* at about this same time. I'd heard somewhere that a sniper was loose in Huntington Woods. My mother cannot confirm this memory, and indeed it seems unlikely. Huntington Woods, the town where I grew up, was an early bedroom community of postwar families who worked in Detroit. Only one square mile, it had a library, an elementary school, a swimming pool, a city hall, and a fire station with two engines. Our house sat on Eleven Mile, the northern boundary. One mile south at the other end was the Detroit Zoo. Sometimes, after dinner, we'd pile in the car and drive over to sit with our windows open and hear the lions roar at feeding time.

This was as dangerous as life got for us in the mid-1950s. The neighborhood joked about the time we moved the block party into the Elliots' basement because of stormy weather and were so busy with martinis and orange pop and the ruckus of eight families in one house that we missed the blaring sirens and emerged hours later to find that a tornado had touched down just outside.

This memory about the sniper is anchored to a vision of lying stiffly on the living room couch in front of our picture window facing Eleven Mile Road. I'd learned that day that a *sniper* was a man who drove around shooting randomly into windows, gunning people down as they played solitaire or read the paper. My parents were out for the evening, and I was trapped inside with a baby-sitter who would not let us leave the house. Perhaps she was the source of the rumor, it occurs to me now.

The heat was debilitating, a cloying humidity, an oppressive, overcast sky. No one else seemed concerned. It was as if this kind of thing happened all the time. Unable to enlist help or stir up any excitement in my brother and sister, I spent the hours between dinner and bed taking precautions—walking on my knees, shimmying under the window on my belly, anything not to be visible to the sniper who might choose our house, might choose me.

I MOSTLY PLAYED with boys. I have some memory of the girl next door and I speaking in tongues with our Barbie dolls, but summer days and winter evenings were spent playing crab attack with Petey and then Stevie in the Peterses' basement, riding bikes with Dougie Isaacs, and most memorably, playing Superman with the Osterlund brothers. I was included in this male fantasy because they needed me to play Lois Lane. While Bobby and Russ took turns being Clark Kent and Jimmy Olsen, my role never varied. My job in whatever scenario our inexhaustible imaginations concocted was to be rescued, but first, I had to be put into terrible danger.

Though we were quite young when this game flourished on our block, I remember an erotic charge to it, or at least a romantic one, far exceeding any passion Lois Lane seemed capable of on

TV. Each time I stepped into this drama, I knew I was about to taste something I would later know what to do with. It was a bumbling concoction of vulnerability and chivalry and also a sadomasochistic dance I was learning to dance with boys. The game required that they be the bad guys first, speak to me roughly, muscle me into the garage and slam the door, hustle me around to the side of the house and into the honeysuckle bushes, an eight-year-old's hand clamped lightly over my mouth. It required that I act afraid.

There was a thrill in the anticipation of this terror each time we began, but I never liked it as much as the part that came next, when Superman would spring from nowhere and ask me if I was all right. There'd be a charge of connection between Russ and me or Bobby and me in this moment, which leaked around the edge of our roles and thrilled me deeply, leading me to hunger for time alone with a boy who was stronger than I, who looked out for me and knew how to save me.

I always felt guilty about these moments of romantic attachment because Russ and Bobby did not reciprocate. They had nothing to say to me most days, did not know what to make of me once the game was over. I was soon hooked on the relationship between danger and romantic attention.

HE WAS HANDSOME in a suburban way: clear eyes, very white teeth, auburn hair falling neatly across his forehead. He looked like a magazine ad my mother might read and dream about for me.

To understand who he was to me, you have to understand the girl I was in high school, in 1968, in the tony suburb into which my family had moved the year before. I think of my first summer in the suburbs as the summer of my banishment. With the dramatic narcissism of adolescence, I equated myself with Kafka's

Joseph K, pulled from his warm bed and thrown into jail for some unidentified crime.

I'd been yanked from my happy life in Huntington Woods and found myself without sidewalks, without friends, and when I entered high school, completely without cachet. Short a car, a wardrobe, expendable income, and practice moving among the moneyed class, I was as good as invisible. I spent my high school years knowing that I could see them, but they could not see me.

When I peer at myself across the distance of three decades, what do I see? A boisterous girl gone suddenly shy, sitting in bed among a huge pile of books and papers. The radio is on—a tube radio that glows at night, tuned to the FM band. Judy Collins is singing "Both Sides Now," and later Leonard Cohen will sing "Suzanne," and then Bob Dylan will make it all a religious experience. Sometimes there is Motown, the poetry of plain talk and sex that black culture brought roaring into my bedroom, making me shake all over the bare wood floors in that house beyond our means, always cold from the heat kept low. What's important here is that when the boy I'll call Thomas entered the scene, I spoke to very few humans, least of all boys.

Thomas sat across from me in junior year algebra. For some reason, he could see me, and I felt immensely grateful. I don't recall having a crush on him. It was more just relief for a bit of conversation. Certainly, he initiated every conversation. I would not have dared. He was too handsome. He was on the varsity soccer team. On Fridays, he'd come to class in a sport coat and tie. All the athletes wore coats and ties on game days. They walked among us with a kind of military formality those afternoons, set apart, readying for battle, tall, cool warriors who knew things we'd never know, who had more important things to think about than the symbolism in *A Streetcar Named Desire*. They deserved our respect. They got out of school early. They were They.

Thomas was quieter than the other jocks, less sure of himself.

He wasn't as smart as I thought he should be, or perhaps he simply wasn't applying himself. I noticed he didn't do the homework. Once he wrote me a note on a set of papers like Russian nesting dolls, one word on each piece of graph paper, the pieces getting smaller and smaller, the last one a single gray square. Put together, the note said: "Help, I'm a prisoner in a Chinese graph paper factory."

Toward the end of the school year, he started bringing thick loose-leaf notebooks to class—a home-study course in stocks and bonds. He wasn't going to go to college, he told me. He was going to start earning money right away. He showed these notebooks to me with tenderness and pride, as if presenting pictures of his family or the dogs he'd loved as a child. I listened with the avidity of the starving, and he redoubled his efforts. I worried that he might pull his desk right across the aisle next to mine and start going through the notebooks, page by page, tedious lesson by tedious lesson. It didn't occur to me that he was starving, too.

A few weeks later, Thomas stabbed a woman thirty-nine times with an ice pick and killed her. There. Explain that. Try explaining it to a shy girl with an overengaged imagination. I understand that a huge quantity of drugs was found in the car he'd stolen. I understand that he was out of his mind the night he stabbed the young hitchhiker thirty-nine times. But I also understand that nearly everything I want to know about that young man is something I do not understand.

I do not understand why he was not in class one day when, the day before, he'd smiled his generous smile and said, "See you tomorrow." I don't understand why he ran away from home just weeks short of graduation, how he ended up on the East Coast, where he got the amphetamines found in his car, who his companion was, why they picked up the young girl, the girl who could have been me, who could have been me if I'd had the spunk to be out hitchhiking, who might have accepted a ride if a nice boy like him had been driving the car.

The rumors about his crime flew around the school, but I was so isolated I heard nothing substantial. I later read the details in the local papers, read of his arrest, trial, and sentence on charges of involuntary manslaughter. What's involuntary about thirty-nine times?

I had no sympathy for him. I wanted him in jail forever. The effect of his crime on me was like the movie I'd scared myself with as a twelve-year-old, in which well-known actors remained hidden behind elaborate and convincing masks until, at the end of the movie, they peeled off the latex to reveal their true identities. I could not trust the nicest male I knew not to stab me with an ice pick. I could not trust myself to know whom to trust.

I put this incident away in precisely the same drawer as the other scraps of troubled knowledge. It did not haunt me. In fact, I nearly forgot it had happened, but as a young woman, I entered the world of male intimacies with wariness. I kept the Summer of Love at arm's length, but my caution was rooted in my unconscious and was therefore endlessly confusing.

In an atmosphere of generalized mistrust, innocent men are stopped and questioned. Everyone waits at the roadblock. You are expected to carry and show identification. It takes the fun out of things. This is the face of reverse oppression. It makes good men furious, and its enforcer is every woman who has ever been made afraid.

A PRETTY YOUNG WOMAN, traveling alone, steps into a motel shower and is stabbed to death. The blood swirls and swirls, beautiful almost, going down.

I saw *Psycho* only once, in high school, on TV, without forewarning or context. To me, Alfred Hitchcock was the clever butler who introduced an offbeat late-night TV series. I had no idea that I would never be able to rid myself of the image of Janet Leigh, safe in her motel room behind a locked door, stepping naked into the shower. *Fool. Psycho.*

Years later, Laura Palmer's shrouded body, bluish lips, and tangled homecoming-queen-hair would bring praise for the film-maker who put her on TV. for us to stare at. How ravishing she looks dead! Hitchcock killed off Janet Leigh before the end of the first reel. *Twin Peaks* was never interested in Laura Palmer. The deaths of these women were not the *point,* I've been told. But I, as they say, *identified.*

THE LAST STRAW was Richard Speck. Whatever seeds of female fear had been planted in my childhood were forced into bloom by the news of eight student nurses in Chicago murdered in their dormitory beds. Fear has made a permanent home in me ever since. Like the roots of the baobab tree in Saint-Exupéry's *Little Prince*, it circles the whole planet; it threatens the existence of the rose.

I was on vacation with my family when I read of the murders. I don't remember having considered the phrase *mass murderer* before, though I'd seen the films of Buchenwald and lost a light part of my heart to the word *assassination.*

To be eligible for this murder, all you had to be was a young woman. A young woman living in a dormitory. I fit the description, and so did my college roommate, Kathleen, daughter of the family we'd vacationed with for many years. I can see us cross-legged on her bed in the house our families rented each year near Lake Michigan. We have the *Detroit Free Press* spread out in front of us, and we are reading aloud, as if to memorize the words (*leukemia, sniper, assassination, mass murderer*). Years later a friend tells me that she got married because of Richard Speck. Right out of college, University of Chicago. Seemed like a wise idea.

. . .

IF THERE WERE childhood rehearsals for female fear, were there also instructions in courage? My mother would be the last to call herself courageous, yet it is to a quality in her character that I ascribe my courage. There were glass mountains to scale and piles of straw to be spun. What kept me from giving myself over to ogres or the mockery of wisecracking crows was the instruction of my mother's best trait. Her curiosity about the lives of others and, therefore, about possibilities available in a life over-shadowed even her own ambitions. To be fair, curiosity was per-haps her response to the seeming impossibility of her own ambi-tions. Still, her example evolved into a dogged hunger with which I marked a trail. Curiosity, then, saved the cat.

A DAUGHTER WAS BORN recently into a friend's fam-ily, a family of boy children, and we celebrated on a wide porch in the midst of a June heat wave. The group included frankly envi-ous mothers of sons, mothers of young girls, weary, cautious mothers of grown daughters, as well as women without children. Baby Maeve spent most of the night in the arms of a former nun who held her with experienced tenderness.

As a group, these were women whose spiritual lives had vital-ity and clarity because they had attended to them. So the evening included not only the singing of Irish lullabies and the soft won-der of girl clothes in box after box, but ritual. In the first, each woman strung a bead onto a necklace for Maeve and offered a piece of advice to the mother and child. *Let her wear whatever she wants. When she gets older, don't be afraid to tell her no. The world is a hard place for a girl.*

Then a woman carrying a sheaf of magician's flash paper and a candle asked each of us to write a wish for the baby based on some-thing we hadn't had, or hadn't had enough of ourselves. We scribbled in silence, in silence ignited the paper into a flare of whirling light on the dark porch. From a distance, an observer would have seen curlicues of fire rise, spin, and vaporize, then have heard a collective, irrepressible gasp at the small spectacle of it.

I decided instantly what I would write on the little paper: *Safety.*

And my wish vanished in thin air, along with all the others. Toward the end of the circle, one of the women broke the pattern and announced her wish before igniting it. *More encouragement and a sex education,* she declared. Then, another woman spoke in the flaring light. *Fearlessness!* I felt an immediate regret, almost a reprimand. *Of course—fearlessness.* That was the proper thing for which to wish. How fearful of me to strike the careful note of safety!

I WAS ONCE scornful of fearlessness. It struck me as a privileged attitude suitable for immature adolescents and male-mythic-Rambo heroism. For women the longing for fearlessness is certainly a longing for freedom, a longing that intensifies in each generation, a longing complicated in our time by AIDS and by increased awareness of date rape. Katie Roiphe is perhaps our loudest voice in expressing this longing. I first read Roiphe in her debut appearance in the *New York Times Magazine* (1993). The cover graphic was a full-page close-up of a woman screaming, her face distorted by a blood red wash of color. The headline read "Rape Hype." I assumed that I would read a critique of the movie-of-the-week sensationalization of rape. Instead, the essay, by the then twenty-five-year-old Roiphe, tried to make a case for fearlessness, arguing that rape prevention efforts are an unnecessary intrusion on women's freedom.

Roiphe asserted that a societal emphasis on safety implies the need for others to act on women's behalf. Safety implies protection of the weak and restriction of the strong-willed modern woman.

Rape speak-outs and campus education programs looked to her like insidious attempts to keep young women afraid. Furthermore, Roiphe suggested that rape does not actually occur as often as we're told. She claimed that inflated statistics—"rape hype"—are concocted by older feminists to scare young women. ("If twenty-five percent of my women friends were really being raped—wouldn't I know it?" she wrote.) In any case, she instructed, most date rape could be prevented by any strong, smart woman up on her self-esteem. *You can't thread a moving needle* is the old adage, I believe. Men have, essentially, no responsibility for rape in this formulation, and that comforts her. Society is not required to contribute to the safety in women's lives and that keeps her feeling free.

It's hard to overstate my reaction to this article. I eventually came to terms with Roiphe and the recklessness with which she dismissed a profoundly important reality. Her desire for autonomy is poignant. I share it. I recognize her impulse to insist on it. Her denial that there's a shark below the surface of the fairy-tale sea reminds me of my desire to return to the apartment to sleep after I was raped. Foolhardy, blind, a child's insistence that the party is not, *is not,* over. I actually began to worry about her, to wonder at the roots of her own fear. Her arrogance seemed a defense against a fear so large it could not even be acknowledged.

I have not fully come to terms with those who continue to invite Roiphe to air her fears by dismissing the experience of others and the statistical evidence. Perhaps these editors are attracted by the "freshness" of her give-it-a-rest point of view. It's a relief, after all, to hand the responsibility for sexual violence over to women. It keeps things lively in the halls of commerce. How provocative to watch the little lady argue that the world is flat, particularly if you've got a warehouse full of rulers to unload. How reckless to address women's fear with a myth of fearlessness.

• • •

RECENTLY, HOWEVER, I acquired an image of fearlessness that I actually can use. I saw the film *Rob Roy* just for the chance to take in the beautiful faces of its middle-aged stars and was surprised to find in it a radical portrayal of rape. In this reasonably decent popular film, Jessica Lange plays Mary McGregor, a woman long married to the local hero portrayed by Liam Neeson. It is sixteenth-century Scotland, and she is busy with the children and the home fires while he's out protecting the village.

The pivotal act of the film is the rape of Mary McGregor by her husband's enemy. The assault is brief, cruel, and devoid of sexual energy. Here, rape is a weapon of war, an accurate characterization of its fundamental brutality. (In 1998, in response to the mass killings in Rwanda, rape was defined for the first time as a genocidal crime in the trial of Jean-Paul Akayesu.)

Safety is not possible for Mary McGregor in this situation, but a form of fearlessness allows her to act. She does not fear what has happened to her so much as what may happen as a result. She takes control of the aftermath, an extremely rare occurrence in film portrayals of rape. She is seen as neither a victim nor a survivor. She's a leader.

Correctly assessing the motivation for the rape—to enrage her husband and inspire revenge—she determines not to tell him. Her reasons have nothing to do with shame and everything to do with wisdom. She communicates this decision to her husband's young protégé, who is present at the scene.

He is reeling from the event, desperate to take action, to see his role model get even. In the most thrilling moment of the film for me, Lange washes her body in the river moments after the rape, her face a blasted landscape of the incomprehensible. Everything is moving fast: the water, her hands, her eyes, the frantic pleas of the protégé. "I won't be able to keep silent," he laments.

"If *I* can do it, so can you." She is fearless in this moment, readying herself to include rape in the movement of her life, eventually even to bear the child who has been created. As I watched her, beautiful in the weariness of late womanhood, I attached myself to her strength, to its lack of drama, its belief in the future despite the disaster of the moment. She was not crazy with anger or grief; she was not frozen with fear or sadness. She was in charge of a life that included passion, marriage, children, rape.

What's missing in this portrayal are the other consequences of trauma, consequences missing from most war stories as well. We rarely see the decades of nightmares, the outbursts of anger, the all-too-common use of alcohol to blot out memories. Perhaps this dimension will eventually be included in portrayals of women of heroism. For now, I am grateful for an image in popular culture that gives female fearlessness a face, not Wonder Woman or Lois Lane, not Thelma and Louise, but a woman with her eyes open to the dangerous world and to the use of her own limited power to act. It is a bit of a fairy tale, but it gave me what fairy tales can offer—images stripped to their essence so we can carry them with us as we shape our own stories.

12

DO I *LOOK* ANGRY?

When feminists say rape is violence, not sex, we mean to say that from our perspective as victims of forced sex, we do not get sexual pleasure from rape; contrary to the rapist's view, the pornographer's view, and the law's view, rape is not a good time for us. This is a valiant effort at cross-cultural communication.

—ANDREA DWORKIN,
"Violence Against Women, It Breaks the Heart, Also the Bones"

EIGHTY PERCENT of marriages don't survive a rape," Dorothy warned us. Interesting, I thought at the time, but irrelevant. We had the marriage we wanted. We were together. Period. Cautiously, as if not to tempt fate, we note our amazement that our sexual relationship has not been disrupted. Then, I begin to cry when we make love. At first the tears feel like simple release, the result of strong feelings, but as they become a consistent presence, they open into a great sadness, causing me to turn away from Tim. We take this, too, in stride. For a while.

September 1982. Am out of touch with happiness. Is it suspect, seductive, connected to sexuality, and therefore too frightening?

By the end of that first summer, a jumpy energy moves me around the house, out of bed, banishing the stunned daze that has characterized my waking hours. I am irritated, irritable, all the time. Tim hooks a canvas bag to the basement ceiling, and I learn to punch it, tentatively, then with pleasure, working myself into a heat of useless fury until even that isn't enough. One night, I wrench it from the ceiling, throw it like a body against the wall, stalking the basement, whispering fiercely, wanting a fair fight, a second chance.

Donna asks me to write an alternative scenario: *What do you wish had happened that night?* Reading it aloud in her office, my voice gathers force. I experience a moment of literary transformation where the power to imagine feels like true power.

> *I meet him standing up. I find my voice right away. Get out of here, I shout, backing him down the hallway. What the hell are you doing in my house? I tear the blindfold from my face and look him straight in the eye, see who he is and make him see me. I throw him against the wall, tell him that his troubles are none of my concern.*

The sound of refusal fills me with longing. Were I to dwell on aggressive images, would I learn to act them out? What if such fantasies became fundamental to my sense of self? How necessary is this for women to learn? Is this what occurs in the psyche of the rapist?

WITHOUT A FACE or name to anchor him in my thoughts, the rapist begins to generalize, to mythologize, and my anger finds other targets. All sexualized images of women begin to look like symptoms of the problem. I become the Carry Nation of the female body. For a brief, intense period, I want bodies to be *invisible*—my own included—or at least not important, not objectified or glorified, not seen. I want women depicted working or thinking, not in their underwear, not with their legs taking up most of the screen.

I begin to prefer loose, plain clothes, flat shoes, flannel night-gowns. I take on a delayed radical education: Susan Griffin, Andrea Dworkin, Riane Eisler. I write a play about Marilyn Monroe and a group of feminist terrorists who spray paint graffiti on offensive billboards in the dark of night. I have no sense of humor, no sense of balance. I see no gray, though I wear it.

Advertising is a constant source of outrage, as is most male humor. Forget MTV. Former pleasures become impossible: the Beat writers I so loved, Henry Miller, edgy movies. Mick Jagger makes me crazy, and I have to skip rap entirely. *Under my thumb, a jagged cut, under my thumb, act right . . .* I switch off the radio while companions in the car still bounce to the irresistible beat. I begin to be hard to entertain.

As if I've gotten a piece of splintered glass in my eye, I view the world through the narrow lens of rage. I see reflections of the rapist's hatred and disregard everywhere. A writer-friend research-ing an article about the landmark antipornography ordinance briefly on the books in Minnesota runs into the full force of my altered perspective one day. A kind and reasonable man, he'd done research and thought hard and come down against the ordinance for reasons of free speech. Knowing me to routinely champion free speech, he innocently outlines his thinking on the phone. But in that period of blind anger, I do not hear reasonable; I do not hear thoughtful. I hear blatant personal betrayal. How can he sanction exploitative images of women? Doesn't he remember what hap-pened to me?

April 1983. I think a great deal of my fear of pleasure comes from the fact that my body was hurt. It's a fragile barrier that keeps death away. After an attack, you are reluctant to rely on it for anything. Somehow, lately, pleasure always threatens to turn into pain.

I was not reasonable, but I was right. Everything I understood in this raw period happened to be true. It was just not the only truth. Powerful, unmediated truths are like straight gin; they can kill you, kill the "you" in you. For me that meant the Audrey Hepburn thing might have to go if the Audre Lorde thing was in place. There wouldn't be room for a Rita Hayworth moment, or the way men's backs look in denim, the way the male gaze, so suspect in translation, can glint with pleasure.

I love some men. I love them dearly and deeply and passionately and madly. But I have no room for the artists, writers, directors, animators, and account executives who use women in their products as sexual objects.

I won't do Disney or Tarantino or Mailer or Lynch. This makes me a bad date in a remarkable number of situations. I was a pain in the lobby after *Pocahontas*. Dull and silent through all the dinner party conversations about *Pulp Fiction*, I was unable to muster a bon mot on its artistic merits because I hadn't seen it. I didn't want to watch rape and bloody death, no matter how amusing they were said to be. I can no longer ignore my body's reaction in deference to my intellect, and sometimes it leaves me feeling a little lonely.

A while back, my friends were gathering on Sunday nights to eat popcorn and watch *Twin Peaks*. It was the most exciting thing on television they told me, brilliant, funny, innovative. I was not watching. I'd seen an episode where the camera lingered over Laura Palmer's dead body and was shocked by how closely one night in my own life resembled that scene. The camera floated in close, circled, caressed her corpse. I was told that this scene was to be repeated again and again throughout the series, a recurring *theme*.

I was suddenly at odds with friends with whom I generally share a sensibility. When I crossed the line between abstract knowledge and the real thing, I experienced a shock. Art has missed the boat. That's not terror up there on the screen, but something orchestrated and composed. Portrayals of violence fail to convey the fragility of skin and bones and the empty horror of a spirit in flight. Real terror is ugly and well worth forgetting, if only you could. Perhaps it's a comfort to imagine that murder can be managed into a palatable package. Perhaps that's why we can yawn and say, "That was pretty good, wasn't it, hon?"

RECENTLY, a colleague lent me a videotape that deconstructs the sexualized violence in music videos. The tape concludes with a remarkable segue between music videos and a scene from *The Accused*, a film based on the highly publicized gang rape in a pool hall in New Bedford, Massachusetts. The transition is deliberately seamless. One moment you're watching a parade of images from videos—blindfolded women, women in chains, lined-up like mannequins, wearing only a guitar and a garter belt, and the next "video" turns out to be a rape scene. Even I was briefly fooled, conditioned by the images into viewing the charge of danger in the pool hall as seductive.

Studies of rapists are frustrating in their lack of conclusiveness, but for a certain percentage of them, those prone to the most violence, inflicting pain is sexually stimulating. "The looks of pain, and anguish and hurt. . . . It's not the sex alone, but the looks on their faces that gets me going," commented a convicted rapist, part of a University of Minnesota study about why some men rape.

Poet Audre Lorde once told a gathering of writers, *You who see, tell the others.* I do see a narcotic dose of woman-hating doled out in art and commerce. It keeps us all a little poisoned, impairing us when we're together as workers, partners, and lovers. In some of us, the dose accumulates, becomes toxic, and shows up deadly in our fantasies, illnesses, and crimes.

• • •

WHEN I FIRST LEARNED about what was being called feminism in the mid-1960s, I found that the word rolled easily off my tongue. Why would I argue with a political movement dedicated to giving me choice and opportunity and money and power? It wasn't hard to see the need for it, but I have never been especially politically or socially active. After anger focused my attention on the darker particulars of sexism, I embraced feminism in a new way. It became my business, not to argue philosophically or agree with fanatically, but to attend to. In this way, radicalized anger is ultimately productive. And the women who have used an experience with violence—sexual, economic, or relational—to transform their perspective have changed the world.

I'D ARRIVED AGAIN at paradox. I'd seen something I couldn't ignore, but I wanted to live in the world with men—with their intensity, courage, humor, and ambition. I didn't want to be separated by what I saw through that narrow lens.

My anger had already contributed to a growing distance in my marriage. When I withdrew sexually, Tim was faced with a strain of guilt by association. Was he somehow accountable for the sins of his gender? How could we engage while I was so withdrawn unless he initiated the seduction? Was that pressure? What is the relationship between erotic aggression and rape? Had the line moved? Would he overstep? He became trapped in one of those undecodable logical fallacies: *A man harmed the woman I love. I am a man. Therefore, I . . .*

I could give Tim no help. My anger was easily triggered in those days, and my instinct was to withdraw, to resist his affection, in fact to fear it. "Even after intimate relations are resumed, the disturbances in sexual life are slow to heal," writes Judith

Herman. "In sexual intercourse, survivors frequently reencounter not only specific stimuli that produce flashbacks but also a more general feeling of being pressured and coerced."

Most surprising to me now is the fact that we were surprised by this. Perhaps it was because our sexual path had always been smooth, and in the first nine months after the rape, it remained relatively undisrupted. We were just beginning to understand that the damage would be uncovered in stages.

When Tim inquired at various agencies about a support group for male partners, he was rebuffed. "We don't have enough funding to take care of the *women* who need us," scoffed one overburdened voice on the phone. *Give me a break*, people in the field seemed to be saying—a rape support group for *men*?

There's greater recognition now for the fact that partners need help when their world has collapsed. The skills it takes to manage the strain that trauma places on a relationship are not common knowledge. This is another consequence of the silence we keep. Blindsided, we become statistics. *Eighty percent of marriages don't survive a rape.*

I have an image from this period in our marriage. It's early spring, *that day* when sitting outside in Minnesota is possible for the first time in six months. There's a greedy hunger for the tactile world, for the surging red tulips, the heady smell of mud and vegetation carried on a load of sunlight. Tim and I are in the backyard, probably working on the vegetable bed, and at some point, we sit down on the back steps just to bask. Tim reaches to draw my body to his so that we can lean against each other in the sun. I refuse him, and his face clouds with hurt and then fury. He can't understand where I've gone to, and I can't explain my need for distance. I feel driven by forces that don't answer my questions. It does not occur to me at this point to direct these questions to my body.

June 1984. I feel lost in the world, reluctant, like I'm taking my time to make up my mind about a suitor. On our trip to Seattle, I met pleasure by the water and by the mountains exactly like an old lover: yes, this is the way we used to be together. I hear Tim's foot on the stair and feel the twin stirrings—no, go away, don't engage me, I cannot be engaged, and yes, put your arms around me, let's dally through this rainy day together.

13

THIRD ANNIVERSARY

August 14, 1984

THE SUMMER of the third anniversary, Tim and I visited friends who live in the sandy woods on Cape Cod. That year I'd written a play and seen it through production, and we'd traveled to Mexico, gathering material for a book we would eventually complete together. I was returning to strength. In August, we joined our friends and their houseguests, a woman and her young daughter visiting from Israel, for dinner. I cannot recall the woman's name, but I remember her prophecy.

Standing in the airy kitchen, we kept the conversation as light as the breeze through the trees. I'd been aware of the approach of the third anniversary, but in the amnesia of vacation, I had not noticed its arrival. Suddenly, as I put my glass to my lips, I remembered that *this* was the day. I whispered it to my friend.

Naomi, the woman from Israel, overheard. She turned to look me steady in the face. The effect was of a high-intensity light suddenly swiveled in my direction, the full force of her spirit given over to me. *You must have a child,* she said with the authority of a seer. *A child will bring your joy back. You must do this.*

I was nearly thirty-three, and the question of motherhood had been much on my mind. Tim wanted to have a child, but I worried about what it might mean for the other loves in my life—writing, travel, solitude, ambition. I'd searched for guidance, but such direct, prescriptive advice struck me as wildly un-American. At least among midwesterners, we respectfully do not tell one another what to do.

Naomi's words framed the question in a new way, as an answer to longings I'd left largely unspoken. Now that I was functioning without nightmares and crippling fear, where was my joy? These two events of the body—its survival of rape and its labor toward a child—later became wrenchingly linked. Yet in that moment, they were brought together in the name of joy.

14

LOVE, LABOR, LOSS

Love

> . . . We hoped
> paradise would be like this, so much green
> spilled into blue, everything unbuttoned
> from gravity, naked, dancing hand in hand.
> —JIM MOORE, "Matisse's *Dance*"

IN THE SPRING of 1985, Tim and I traveled to the Greek islands. That journey eventually led to the birth of our son, and it began with a dream. A friend who shared my name and my questions about motherhood saw me standing in a green field wearing a long white dress and a big straw hat, holding a baby. Though I am certain the dream spoke more to her fate than mine, I left for Greece hoping that I would return pregnant.

WE ARRIVED in Delphi late in the afternoon to find flowers blooming in blue buckets at our hotel, a river of olive trees winding down to the bay far below. The sun was coating the tops of the trees; its late magic draped the legendary mountains in shadow. We headed down the asphalt highway toward the site where a procession of altars was visible staggering up Mount Parnassus. But the shrine was closed for the day. Across the highway, down toward the valley of olive trees, was the less-celebrated Temple of Athena. I knew nothing about the Temple of Athena, but I'd read up on Delphi.

Originally a shrine to the Earth Mother, Gaea, it became Apollo's shrine, so the story goes, after he killed the python that protected it. From then on, the oracle's prophecies were delivered by a priestess who entered a trance state. Many of her pronouncements were recorded, particularly as they related to military strategy. In 572 B.C. the oracle told the king of Lydia that if he crossed the river Halys, he would destroy a great kingdom. Obeying, he crossed the river and was defeated by the Persians, thus destroying his *own* kingdom.

One of my favorite childhood books was *Half Magic* by Edward Eager. It told of children who found a magic coin capable of granting half a wish. How the equation of desire and satisfaction was calculated in each of their wishes was the real magic of the book. The wish behind our agreement to make Delphi our one sojourn on the Greek mainland was unspoken. The faithful part of our frightened hearts sought a miracle, a return to ease with the world and each other.

Though I'd sworn allegiance to logic long before, I retained from childhood an openness to magic. Perhaps the oracle still seeped a diluted power into the mountain air that would make me understand what to do about children, faith, sexuality. I thought this might mean an insight, an aphorism springing fullbodied from my forehead. Yet, the miraculous occurred, so far as I can tell, down below, at the Temple of Athena, after-hours.

· · ·

THE TEMPLE OF ATHENA, we discovered from the small wooden sign, was also closed, but here we could jump over the wooden gate, and we did so without much discussion. Picking our way down the rocky path, we were silent, perhaps sobered by our felonious behavior, perhaps by a sacred tension in the landscape. There was not much to see. Piles of dark gray column shards were heaped on the ground, as if work had stopped yesterday or fifty years ago. A round stage was intact, the Doric columns which once ringed it partially restored.

My pulse quickened as we wandered about the deserted temple. The air seemed heavy, full of presence, as if we were being watched. I picked wildflowers from the hillside sloping away from the temple, gathering a huge bouquet very quickly. The motion of bending toward this color, this shape, felt like a dance to match the fading light.

Then, with the sun skimming the tops of the olive groves stretching far below, in a silence so deep I shed the inhibitions that stood guard on my sadness, we found ourselves together in the long grass. Without words, we made real love as dusk crept over the mountain. I was amazed at the ease I felt, how my body flowed toward Tim as it used to. Pleasure, here under Athena's olive trees, seemed unthreatened by pain. Persephone would not be punished for her flower gathering, never be abducted by Pluto, never be sent below to taste the dark fruits.

I rose giddy and delighted, and we crept back up the hillside to the temple site, half-expecting a minotaur or the goddess herself to mete out punishment for our pleasure. How could she be angry with us, I argued, racing round and round the marble altar, throwing flowers. I mistakenly believed us to be in the temple of the goddess of *love*, but that would be *Aphrodite*, I would discover later, Aphrodite whom we'd invoked with our suddenly effortless passion. Athena is the warrior goddess of the city, perfectly capable, it turned out, of chastising transgressors.

"We should get going," Tim urged, gesturing toward the sudden disappearance of the light. We scrambled up to the road, turning back toward the small town of Delphi perhaps half a mile down the highway. Abruptly, we were in complete darkness. A solid black curtain had descended over the mountain. No streetlights, no lights of any kind. A wind whipped up behind us out of nowhere, flattening our hair, rustling the trees, pushing at us on the road. We held on to each other, blinded and unsteady under the wind's sudden force. I was conscious of the hillside dropping off to our left, of trying to stay in the middle of the road, and of a cold terror that any car roaring around these curves would find us squarely in its path.

We crept along in a focused silence broken by only two sounds. We remembered the sounds later and agreed perfectly about their character. First came the brief and distinctive hoot of an owl. A bit later, very close by, the delicate giggling of women. We prepared to meet these women momentarily on the road, and I was relieved at the thought, but no one ever emerged. We never heard footsteps nor voices, just a tripping, musical laugh in the air like a woman in love.

Eventually, around a curve, the starry lights of Delphi appeared down below. Struck by the oddity of the incident, I consulted my copy of Edith Hamilton's *Mythology* after we returned to our little hotel. Athena, the virgin goddess, is symbolized by the olive tree, the wind, and the owl. Aphrodite, the goddess of love, is worshipped at Delphi and known by her sweet, mocking laughter.

I'M SURE THERE IS an explanation for what happened on the road to Delphi. Someone like Stephen Jay Gould could probably cite phenomena to account for the owl, the wind, the laughter. I prefer the implication of a powerful mystery, because, for the rest of that month and beyond, I was restored to pleasure. The curve of the islands, the salty Aegean, the closeness of food and drink to ocean and field—octopus, olive, retsina, fig—the erotic was obvious in everything.

We slept late, lay in each other's arms, turned toward the breeze. I learned to join the European women in baring my breasts at the beach. We learned to crave the licorice bite of ouzo at sunset, fat-drenched yogurt in the morning. The trip unfolded like an object lesson in sensuality, a high dose of earthy glory for the grief-stricken, the faithless, the heartbroken, the frozen.

THE SOFT ROCKS in the bay have eroded into provocative shapes—breasts, buttocks, enormous hips. After swimming, I lick my own skin, letting it salt my tongue. Lunch at a beach-side taverna, eavesdropping on a young Greek-American and two elderly German ladies. "You must drink wine if you are to talk philosophy," he says and proceeds to drink and talk in detail about using olive oil as a tanning agent.

Inside a courtyard smelling of jasmine, a bearded priest in robes crosses his arms and grins at us. A woman in Cretan black seems to stand in attendance for eight tan tourists seated around a table. We ask about a room. She gestures toward the table. I brush against a tree that looks like an overfed maidenhair fern blooming with red-throated flowers the color of butter.

We are brought glasses of a sweet wine with a peppermint tang. (We later learned it was made from roses.) A few of the Germans speak English and translate occasionally. They have stayed in this tiny village for two weeks. This is their last night. We have found a special place, they tell us. The priest is Poppa, his wife, Maria.

Maria brings a plate of squash flowers stuffed with rice. She hugs us with familial affection. Poppa appears with a honeycomb the size of a washboard and standing over the table, cuts chunks for each of us. I suck the honey from the waxy comb. It flows like water, like sunlight, down my throat. Maria brings a plate of warm, runny goat cheese. Murmurs and sighs, "Ah, Maria, it's very good tonight." I feel as if I am in my own dream of Greece. The light fades, the talk surrounds us like a slow river. Poppa shows us to our room, the top floor of the house where he was born. Later we swim naked in the warm Mediterranean Sea.

AFTER GREECE, I regained some of the capacity for pleasure that was stolen from me just as my Russian box, my bracelet, and my watch had been. By the next summer, I was pregnant, and we prepared to celebrate the birth of a baby as well as the publication of the novel I'd been working on the night the rapist broke into our apartment. We did not foresee that the darkness would return, ushered back into our lives by a difficult labor, nor that it would extinguish the light in our eyes. We did not foresee that we would lose each other.

Labor

DRAGONFLY: *it's a gigantic project of a body, intricate with engineered, iridescent wings. My son's dinosaur books name the Emperor Dragonfly as one of the elders of the planet, still with us from the Jurassic Age. I watch this flying circus land on a birch tree behind me. No wonder they've survived the centuries. They're always copulating, in midair, on the water, right here! I make a sketch in my notebook.*

Looped together, they are a dusty blue oval. The male holds to the tree with impressive strength, his head pointed toward the sky, and the female arches her body beneath him. She curves nearly in half so that his blue-and-black-checkered tail brushes her upper body, completing the circle. Their wings are invisible, and then are cords of silver thread in the random sunlight, made of some crushable strength, some beautiful and practical marriage of structure and grace. The wind lifts the circle they make and plays with it like a leaf, and then they settle down again, their beautiful colors flashing, their large flatish heads spotted with gold.

They remain together a long time. As I watch them, I remember conceiving our son. I have told him many times that he is made of the sun and the sky. This suits him as a description of his coloring and his personality, helps explain the crystalline blue of his eyes. But I mean it more literally. He was conceived in the sunlight, on an island in Lake Superior, his mother lying in the deep, soft sand of late afternoon, his father circling above. The high sun and the June sky and the racing clouds swirled in my open eyes. I heard the waves and felt a singular racing of the elements above and then through me. I felt the presence of God. I loved our bodies in the circle, in the hands of love.

Afterward I ran down the beach in my black dress and my bare feet, letting the cold water lap onto my ankles. I ran a long way without effort, without straining for breath or feeling the pull of gravity on my muscles. I am not a runner, so the effect was of a miraculous intervention. At the time I thought, How full of joy I am, how it courses through me. And the lines of the poet came back to me: Lucky life. Oh lucky life. Oh lucky lucky life. Lucky life.

ANDRE'S BIRTH was dramatic, in contrast to his days of becoming. I spent my pregnancy in a state of quiet astonishment that, at thirty-five, my body could surprise me so. I was still standing apart from my physical being, but this time as an admirer, curious, impressed. I have never been athletic, but I experienced pregnancy with the kind of prideful glory that others find in running or weight lifting.

At the same time, I felt I could take no credit. *I* was not making the fingernails. I took my cues from the same inner voice full of instructions that I'd heard the night I battled with the rapist. *Eat now, eat meat, more mashed potatoes.* Both events remain fundamentally mysterious and fundamentally spiritual.

Labor began in the parking lot of the paint store. We were frantic to complete the renovation of our attic, and I'd spent the last month of my pregnancy at home, revising my novel, looking at paint chips, napping in the afternoon. Every day, our carpenter would assess the size of my belly and the vacancy in my smile and work a little faster, terrified that he might have to deliver the baby himself some afternoon.

*P*EOPLE HAVE BEGUN *to stare at me on the street. "Shall I bag these light?" the grocery clerk asks. I've begun to imagine I stand for something, that if I showed my belly to a man about to commit a crime, he would stop in shame. I feel as if the day you arrive, the world will burst into flower-greening, humming, never to die back again. Perhaps just a bit grandiose of me, since picking something up off the floor is a major project these days. Let me go on record against women making national security decisions in the last month of pregnancy.*

MY MIDWIVES had been full of dreamy advice: have a glass of wine to relax yourself, take a bath, bring music, a focus object, invite your pals. We did all this, but we didn't drink the bottle of champagne until Andre's first birthday when I toasted my sister and our friend Mary for their willingness to witness what rather quickly shaped up as an ordeal. Cancel the hors d'oeuvres. And the focus object.

The untold detail of many birth stories is how close women feel to death. In our happiness about the results, we often skip over the process. We gaze into the future and count its toes. But labor brings women into the passageway between being and non-being. Though our eyes are on life, the path clearly goes in two directions. These days, in some parts of the world, the actual risk of death has become quite small. But the door *is* open. Babies die and women die, and even in a hospital progressive enough to take a step "back" toward allowing autonomy, death slips in the door, an unmistakable presence hovering in the corners of the room.

I needed to tell the story of labor in much the same way as the story of rape. I knew a number of women who were delivering children, and when we exchanged stories, I was surprised by how many had not spoken of their labors before, and by the rush of emotion released in them when they did. I am careful now to marvel not only at the new baby in a mother's arms, but also to marvel at her. I ask pointed questions, inviting the details.

But there was one part of my story that I didn't include in my recitation of the thirty-six hours, the failure to progress, the roller-coaster pitocin ride. I held the key to a mystery for years before I could fit it to its lock. The mystery I had stumbled on was this. Early in labor I began to have flashbacks to the experience of rape. I remember less of a movielike quality than the term *flashback* suggests. I remember visceral panic—cellular, I might say— an eerie sensation of being two places at once. It made no sense, and I was unwilling to give it any room, discounting its occurrence until years later.

I AM IN BED in the birthing room, my labor mild and manageable, talking on the phone to my mother. At the same time, I feel as if I have returned to the bloody bedroom near Lake of the Isles, and my life is in danger. This sensation flutters up like a worry. I decide not to mention it to my mother and dismiss it like a rogue spell of dizziness.

I walk, breathe, rock in rhythm with contractions that blot out the room, like lovemaking strong enough to isolate you from everything but the experience itself. I take baths, Tim pouring warm water over my belly to ease the pain. *Nubain, Nubain,* I chant, loving the gentle drug that helps me stay calm, the midwife who rubs my back and whispers encouragement through the night, orders Tim to get some sleep.

In the morning, discouraged and exhausted, I am sent home as labor weakens and I fail to dilate. At home, I am blasted out of bed by massive contractions and come rocketing back to the hospital. A new midwife is on duty, and she begins to give me reason to hate her. She is brusque, silencing my moans, *Come on, now, it's not so bad.* Soon she has tethered me to a bank of machines, internal and external monitors, which restrain my movements.

Eventually, she hooks up a catheter, and I feel not assisted but invaded. I feel tied to the bed. The flashbacks return. I order myself to refuse the associations, but the old panic insinuates itself into the room. I identify the source clearly—trapped, expected to cooperate, somehow doomed to accept what is happening to me. *I've been here before.*

I am furious about this. I have been longing for the experience of giving birth to this baby. I remember thinking *I will not have the best thing that's ever happened to me linked with the worst. I won't have it.* Instead of asking to have the monitors removed, I decide to banish the rape from the birthing room. With this, I doom myself to the wrath of a buried truth.

It has been more than twenty-four hours, and I am determined to deliver vaginally. I suspect that at age thirty-five I might not have another chance. I tap all my resources, though a part of me is afraid I won't have any stamina left to push this baby out. The nurses counsel me to consider a cesarean, but I won't do it.

My midwife is elsewhere most of the time, returning just long enough to seem frustrated with my lack of progress. My strength diminishes. She decides to give me pitocin, a jump start that kicks off a second night of labor and leaves me feeling depraved and stripped of all bravery, reduced to begging for morphine.

Something shattering is happening, not like a glass breaking, more like the earth heaving open, a volcano breaking the surface. Huge. You will never be the same. I silence mind and spirit, strap them atop the bucking horse, use the power left me to try to stay on. There is no cunning in this, no strategy, no plan. It's like being washed overboard in a storm: endurance counts, and strength. Faith is helpful, too, but where are the signs of progress, the reassurances that everything is going according to plan? Where is everybody? From somewhere outside me comes the sound of a woman screaming. It isn't me, but why isn't this in the newspapers?

I HAVE A CLEAR IMAGE of the young doctor who enters the room to consult about the shot of morphine. Standing over me, he talks so slowly to the midwife. He pivots and looks out the window. I am ready to kill him. He holds the possibility of relief, and though I am wretched, like a beggar or a dog in the street, he seems not to notice. He takes forever to return. The morphine takes forever to work. I swim a night sea of near unconsciousness as my body struggles to open. Dream babies drift across my cloudy landscape, fusing one into the next as if computer-generated, mathematically precise. I never dilate past five. I dimly remember glimpsing Tim, gulping down a bowl of soup in the corner, looking panicked.

I check out. My eyes remain closed to devote myself to the delirium of consuming pain. When I surface, hours have gone by, and I don't have what it takes to do this. I cannot go on. Again I collide with the night six years before when I felt so cold and tired, without anyone to help me, with life and death at stake.

Finally, late in the afternoon of the third day, everything speeds up. The monitors tell of trouble, and a needle is suddenly in my spine. It's an emergency. I am pushed without ceremony into what strikes me more as madhouse than operating room. The walls are milk-of-magnesia pink, someone is shaving me for surgery, no one is telling me anything I can use, Tim is somewhere behind my head, and a confused swirl of people are shouting to one another as if never having done this before.

They have, of course. They know exactly how fast they have to move to save the life of the little boy who leapt and dove inside me trying to arrive, meeting a resistance I would only later understand, and in the process tying his umbilical cord into a "true knot." When they lift him beautiful from my belly, they marvel at the feat he has performed, and I nurse him just long enough to recognize him as family before passing out from exhaustion. He spends the first hours in our world being rocked by his father and his aunt Julie while his mother journeys back from the brink we've come to together.

The long vertical scar out of which he emerged tells of how close we came, of the surgeon's need to act *now*. For a long time, I hated it. It scared me and spoke of more pain, more invasion. After labor, as I drew away from my body a second time, I felt only sadness when I looked at that scar, until a good man taught me to love it, to see in it my beautiful boy, to notice how like a river it is, lapping across my belly.

AFTERWARD, the doctor could only shrug her expert shoulders, saying she had no explanation with which to salve my disappointment. I forgot about the intrusion of rape memories as quickly as possible. I dismissed them as odd, but not significant. It was years before I recognized that labor may have stimulated a bodily memory of rape and closed my body down.

We have come to understand the veteran who jumps into foxhole readiness when hearing a car backfire. In just such a way, labor may have triggered the fear responses still stored in my body. Again, research indicates that this deeply ingrained response pattern is a *physiological* process brought on by changes in the body after trauma. According to Judith Herman:

> The traumatic moment becomes encoded in an abnormal form of memory, which breaks spontaneously into consciousness, both as flashbacks during waking states and as traumatic nightmares during sleep. Small, seemingly insignificant reminders can also evoke these memories, which often return with all the vividness and emotional force of the original event.

Six years after Andre's birth, I was led to Lynn Madsen, a therapist who knew how to read the story of my labor. Though we met for many months, our most powerful conversation was our first. I outlined my history, but instead of murmuring sympathetically, she finished my sentences.

"You're a textbook case," she said. "What we're discovering is that women who have experienced rape or incest often experience traumatic labors. However, if they are prepared for the frightening associations that may impede their labor, they can have normal deliveries."

In her book *Rebounding from Childbirth*, Madsen details her own difficult labors and offers advice to women who face or have already experienced traumatic births. While I did everything I knew to deliver Andre, I did not accommodate the memory I carried *in my body* of the last time I'd felt trapped and terrified. Had I been coached to acknowledge the associations, I might have been able to reverse my body's remembered reactions and open the door to allow our baby to pass through.

Loss

THE LABOR EXPERIENCE had consequences that reverberated into our family's future. I believe it triggered a post-traumatic stress reaction, a reprise of the aftermath of rape. Sex became painful, touch confusing, physical contact exhausting.

Preoccupied by the shock and work of motherhood, I attributed my altered mood entirely to hormones. It didn't occur to me that this second withdrawal from the body might be related to the first. I saw time as linear. After Greece, I'd felt "cured." Leslie Marmon Silko has described time as a tortilla, a circular plane that allows events to be revisited again and again. I experienced this time travel in my body's reactions, but I was unable to address the problem because I did not understand its source.

Private griefs and haunts were triggered for Tim as well, and we began to play an unhappy game of avoidance and blame. When we did find comfort in each other's arms, I often ended up in tears. Intense feelings of any kind lapped right into the pool of old grief I was trying to ignore.

WE MOTHERS *are newborn with no one to care for us. We need our mothers and our mother's mothers. Men won't do just now. We have frightened them with our bodies and our transformation. They become hunters and gatherers for a while, hoping we'll change back to the women we were before.*

We can't bear to be separate from the babies. A part of our body has been wrenched from us with a significant amount of pain. One thing I know about pain is that it's there to make you think. But we are modern women and the world says, Up on your feet, girls! We jump and then sit in our cars in front of the day care center and let

*our shoulders heave as we drive away from the sight of our hearts, as
someone once said, walking around outside our bodies.*

*At the end of the day we return like lovers from the sea. We cover
their bodies with kisses and try to rejoin flesh to flesh. Our boundaries
are shot. We are in love and in mourning all at the same time, and we
are not ourselves, we tell one another. The men know and feel betrayed.
They hadn't expected this loss, hadn't agreed to it. No matter how much
we love them, the babies come first. That fact remains unspoken and
flares in the heated night. We hire a baby-sitter so that we can fight.*

Suddenly, we were in trouble. We fought, disappointed
in each other, and in ourselves. We put our energy into becoming
parents. We held on, swinging from terrible behavior to tenderness
and belief in fairy tales.

Tim's letters to me from this period read like a cry: he is desperate not to leave me, not to feel I've left him. He asks me to come
back, in spirit and in body, but I don't know how. The slightest
touch or invitation to intimacy seems a threat. I hear demands I
can't accommodate; react with anger, with retreat. As Tim's deep
hurt flares into rage, I began to have other reasons to avoid him.

*It snowed last night—six heavy inches on the tulips and
the buds of lily and iris. Upstairs, crying, I kept thinking: a late storm
killed everything in the garden. Last night after we fought, I drove off
into the snowstorm, wondering who I could talk to, and realized I
wanted to talk to him, the person I was driving away from. I drove
around and around Lake of the Isles, numb, except when a memory
would bring tears, a pang of welcome feeling. I drove around and
around and around, grateful for a calm and beautiful circle to circle,
until I tired and took my sense of exile home with me.*

· · ·

Finally, when Andre is nearly five years old, we separate. I cannot begin to sort out the threads that wove themselves into the shroud in which we buried our marriage. Some of the most important components are not mine to tell. The story of the end of our marriage is larger than the story I am telling here. Whatever else defeated us, the failure of our marriage retains the aspect of tragedy for me. I know how much the ordeal of surviving the rape stole from us. There are days when I believe that our marriage could have survived if we'd been able to reclaim sexual joy a second time. And there are days when I am certain it was never that simple.

Morning—*the room lightens as I sit in the wicker chair in the bedroom where I used to nurse Andre. I am mourning the loss of morning noises. Sounds drift up from downstairs: Tim kidding with Andre, Saturday cartoons, the teapot whistling.*

I want to record how Andre has been this last week since we decided to separate. He seems to know we are moving apart though we have told him nothing yet. He clings to Tim, wants a picture of the three of us. He worries about the house running away, the towels running away. He will not remember very much about these years with a mother and a father together. I am sorry, dear boy. Will you hear me someday? Will you know how hard we tried?

The years of separation were made of a grief more acute and prolonged than any I had suffered before. In some ways, the rape had taught me how to grieve. I was better at it this time, which meant I was worse. I remember waking up alone in bed, already in tears, tears that must have begun flowing in my dreams. I remember staring at a sliver of a moon on the freeway and hearing the saying in my head, *Old moon's in the arms of the new.* I broke into sobs for my lost life, as hidden and huge as the old moon. The new one seemed so pale.

I still suffer from invasions of memory, when an image from our life together is suddenly present, ringing with the charge the experience carried at the time, undiluted by anger or distance or the years. Last month, I remembered the yellow clapboard walls of a diner in Toronto where we went the summer we tried to immigrate to Canada. We were disappointed in the way our country was behaving in 1974 and hoped to find jobs in Toronto. Our job-hunting day would start and end on stools at the counter in this unremarkable little spot.

When the memory returned, it was complete: low, slanting sun turning the walls to apricot, men's voices, the smell of onion and fried meat, my ridiculous high-heeled shoes and sore, blistered feet, my temporary sense of belonging as I drank coffee from a stout cup the color of vanilla ice cream.

There is a stab of loss on the other side of these recollections as fresh as the memories themselves. It is as if a large wave has crashed across the bow of a boat. There is an immediate, shocking pleasure in an image of Tim's head slightly cocked to hold the fullness of his smile or a memory of the deep fawny fur of his chest. And then the loss stings all the way down. The boat pitches and slows and is awash for a moment in crosscurrents. A wail might move through me if I'd permit it, for my lost world, an old happiness, the possibilities of a family life with Andre.

A few years later, I will work with a woman who teaches me to wail. One winter afternoon she will tuck a blanket around me on a massage table. She will ask me to visualize Tim, and I will close my eyes and see us standing on the shore of an ocean. She will ask me to walk down that shore and away from Tim. I will refuse. I will begin to cry. She will begin to sing, a high and moaning wail like the sound of all mourning, a sound so old and true I will feel connected beyond my own sadness to sadness.

15

ELEVENTH ANNIVERSARY

August 14, 1992

THE FLOOD OF WORDS that began last year on the tenth anniversary is matched this year by quiet. Only Andre in the bathtub this morning moved me toward reflection, a pause at the end of the free fall of this year.

I'm as long as the tub, he announces, and I tell him I will write that down, make note of the day Andre became as long as the tub. He puts on the orange goggles and flippers I bought him for this first summer we are alone.

The water ingests the morning light, turns milky like ice. The sun reflecting off the water dances on the wall, and we watch its flickering presence a long time. *It's magic, Mama,* Andre says, and I say, *Yes, the sun is dancing with the water.* We notice that the pattern changes with Andre's movements, and he is part of the dance. I feel like I'm in a children's book, but it's a lovely moment.

As he dives, I remember his recent efforts at painting, the careful, definite strokes he makes. At five, he is capable of a solemn, quiet authority that gives me a glimpse of how old he is inside, how seriously he takes himself, as I did at his age. I was not a child in my own eyes but an adventurer, already alone, star of my own story, called upon to undertake difficult and serious tasks beyond the understanding of others. He is *diving* in the tub. His experiments with food coloring and soap and Cheerios are *science*.

Living in two households, it will be up to him to make sense of what he's given by his parents. Last summer when Andre was afraid of the neighborhood cat, I saw how differently we instruct him. I knelt down on the grass and told him not to be afraid, tried to convince him that the cat would not harm him. Tim, up on a ladder cleaning the gutters, listened, then called to him. "Go get your power ring." Andre lit up with the idea, raced inside, and returned with the plastic ring and an easy sense of confidence around the cat.

It will be more difficult now, my son, more difficult for us all, but this morning you spun in the bathtub's racing light, and I was lifted by your buoyant heart.

I love August in this house for the leggy cosmos in the front garden tottering on their stems, a visual wind chime. The western sun is heavy at 5:00 P.M. It is the end of summer. I have not felt it so acutely before.

16

YOUR AURA'S GOT HOLES IN IT

This ability to touch and be touched is the simple ability
to love, so hard to save because hope is so hard to save,
especially when it must coexist with knowledge.

—ANDREA DWORKIN, *Intercourse*

W E LIVED APART for three years, parenting our son
jointly, spending more time in therapy together than in laughter.
During this time, I wanted desperately to repair our marriage, for
myself and for Andre. I threw the *I Ching*, threw money at therapists, threw myself into EST-like boot-camp-for-the-psyche week-
ends, threw in with twelve-step meditations and support, threw out
pleas, prayers, and demands. But we remained in our corners, Tim
reduced to rage, and I without my body, without my heart.

Humbled by our failures, I went to St. Paul to see a psychic.
She was a friend of a colleague, I told myself to calm the slightly
appalled voice in my head. What was there left to lose, other than
my respect for myself as a rational being?

W E MEET in the third floor of her home, surrounded by
books and her dogs curled on the floor like guardians. She looks
and behaves like a totally normal person, only a bit more graceful

and reserved than the people I move among every day. She tells me she is clairvoyant, that she works with images, that she is about to enter a trance state to scan the twelve major chakras of my body.

What?

I ask her to go over that for me. I've kept this kind of knowledge at arm's length since I quit being interested in recreational drugs. She tells me that chakras are energy crossroads, like joints in the physical body. Hundreds of them are superimposed on and through the body, but visualizing the twelve major points will allow her to check my emotional, physical, and spiritual health. This doesn't help me much, but I'm in no position to get in her way.

Her first words after closing her eyes concern Tim. "You've brought your husband with you," she says. "You're wearing his energy like a coat. I'm going to ask his spirit to leave the room."

I wait as, apparently, she does this, and we proceed.

"Your aura looks shot full of holes," she says with some distress. And then, "What are you doing to stay grounded in your body?"

"Nothing," I admit. *But what's this got to do with my body? My spirit is broken.*

"Get some exercise," she commands. "Get a massage."

Reasonable advice. *Didn't need a psychic to tell me that.*

She gives me two hours of interesting things to think about, nothing that relieves me or answers my questions about my marriage, but I leave the session feeling quietly better. I drive directly across town to meet a friend, and on the freeway, I feel visually awake. Objects appear distinct from one another, three-dimensional, and saturated with color. I notice the smoke stacks off I-94 billowing the "white flags of winter chimneys," Joni Mitchell once described. I also notice that I've allowed something beautiful to reach me. For weeks, I'll feel cleaned out and running smooth, as if I've had a tune-up.

When I meet my friend directly after the session, I notice a change in her appearance. "What's up?" I ask. "You look so happy. You're almost glowing."

"I've started getting massages," she tells me, pleased with herself, definitely glowing.

In most things, I am known to be slow. But by this time, I've learned not to ignore stunning synchronicity. I call my friend's masseuse despite the fact that she might be moving to Arizona, make an appointment, and my life begins to move.

At first, massage makes me nervous. Up until this point, I have operated as if my body were a storage shed for my mind. I've paid it almost no attention. It has done its spectacular trick—produced a child—and I am generally healthy. No running, yoga, or aerobics for me. I like to live in my head, and take my body to the beach once in a while.

I stay partially clothed during the first few massages. As Kristen loosens my head, neck, shoulders, stomach, hands, feet, back, thighs, calves, I tell her a bit of my story. Then odd things start to happen. When she massages my feet, I battle tears. And what about the clutch in my chest when she pulls the tension from my fingers? Isn't massage like getting a manicure, a nice thing to do for yourself, a perk for athletes in the locker room? Why these strong feelings?

Eventually Kristen explains that because of my history, she'd like to try something she calls "energy work." *Here we go.* Reluctantly, I agree to lay facedown while she stands beside me. Her hands never touch my body; yet, quite soon, I feel heat on my skin. It's not subtle, it's hot. Then, I'm crying.

"I'm crying," I report.

"Yes," she says, "I felt the sadness myself just a moment ago."

She felt the sadness? I'm skeptical, yet I've come to trust this woman, so I decide to let my curiosity lead the way. "But I don't know *why* I'm crying," I mutter into the massage table. In truth, I don't care. Tears are welcome in these agonized, thoughtful days. And these are the easiest tears I've ever cried.

I am without any way to evaluate what's going on, so we just go on. As she shifts her hands over regions of my body, strong feelings rise and crest and melt away. When it's over, I can only compare it to a killer therapy session, but without the hangover of memory or insight. Just the relief. *The gravy.*

WHEN FRIENDS ASK why I seem happier, I can't answer. I'm not about to say *Someone's hands are making it easy for me to cry.* I feel uncomfortable enjoying the results of something I can't explain. Is this just resistance to the new, the way "shrinks" were once thought exotic? I ask Kristen if she will talk with me about energy work.

Her language is a problem for me right away—*energy field, vibration levels, right intention.* I thought I was getting *massages.* I sense that our conversation is as frustrating for her as it is for me. On her part, it's like trying to describe television to someone who doesn't accept the idea of electricity. In fact, I have no actual understanding of how electricity works—let alone radio waves or cell phones. I accept it *because* it works. In the end, I'm more interested in the possible than the probable, in what the road to Delphi embodied rather than how it might be explained.

Kristen believes traumas are often remembered *only* in the body because of the effects of shock, what psychologists might call disassociation. In Kristen's view, trauma is registered in the body at a high level of energy vibration. By adding her energy to mine, she returns my body to the level of vibration at which the trauma occurred, allowing the body's stored memories to be released and the accompanying feelings to be consciously reexperienced.

I don't know what to make of any of this. I certainly don't experience energy work any differently as a result of these explanations. I only know the difference it makes in my future. I continue to get massages every week or two. It has replaced talk therapy in my budget because, in living with post-traumatic stress, I've found that I need to be as aware of sensation as I am of thought. Otherwise, I can go for a long time being thirsty without drinking, stiff without stretching, awake without seeing how the winter smoke looks like a flag against the sky.

*F*EET ARCHED OVER SAND; *knees on moss; thighs a spring-board for tumbling; hipbones when I'm thin; rivery scar, portal of emergence, emergency; hillocks of stomach; breasts when nursing; lungs when I remember them; my shoulders bared, my neck arched for stars; mouth in repose; tongue on sugar and lime; the smell of hot meat and fruit; wind in my hair, a watery fur.*

*M*Y WORK WITH KRISTEN prepared me to take a second step. When a therapist recommended that I call a "body worker," I didn't ask many questions.

"I don't give massages," Mary warns on the phone.

Then what do you do? I think, anticipating just a more rigorous version of energy work.

My first lesson with Mary also involves the need to set aside my native language—judgment, words, logic—and accept the possibility of communication through sensation, image, intention.

"Describe how you are feeling in your body," Mary suggests as I lie fully clothed on a massage table.

What is she talking about? I am unable even to make up something.

She presses me.

"All right, I don't feel great."

"No judgments. Stick with descriptions. Aren't you a writer?" she teases.

Gritting my teeth, I indulge her. "I'm tired," I offer. "I have a bit of an ache in my back."

This is a start, but it's a slow one. I can tell by the number of times we return to this simple question. For weeks we practice identifying sensation, and I learn to distinguish it from feeling and thought. I hate being remedial, but eventually I can detect tightness in my lower back, the pressure of tears behind my eyes, an insistent urge to stretch my legs. My knees are heavy with sadness, and there seems to be a shut-off valve at my pelvis, deadening my left leg. Mary places her palms flat against the bottom of my feet and I am suddenly crying. Yet behind the tears are no stories, no old hurts, or lagging memories.

Mary encourages me to physicalize my thoughts and feelings. "Box up your husband's things," she advises. "Feel what it's like to inhabit the house alone." A friend offers to help me repaint my living room. We remove a lifetime of objects from the walls, rearrange the furniture. Afterward, we sit in the darkening room and I weep miserably. I'm not ready. We put everything back.

"Walk with your feet," Mary tells me, assigning a bit of homework. "Feel the ground when you walk."

Walk with your feet, I repeat to myself like a riddle, clomping around until I begin to notice a connection between my feet and the ground, a taffylike tug. Gravity.

Next Mary teaches me to "locate a center of energy and move it mentally into every cell." As I try to execute this totally abstract assignment, I begin to feel light, as if floating a few inches off the massage table where we do our work. Then she asks me to draw this energy back to my solar plexus. I pretend to do so, ever the good student, mentally rolling my eyes. I experience a sensation of deflation, as if all lightness has left my limbs. I ignore my thoughts about suggestibility, about the power of my imagination. I *recognize* this heaviness.

"This feels like sadness," I say.

"Try allowing your sadness to exist in a body filled with strength and light," Mary advises.

What?

"You don't have to let sadness fill up your whole body."

I am reminded of Algebra II. Nod, listen hard, do as much of the homework as you can. I go through the motions but again find myself struggling with the impotence of language in this realm. During the year and a half I work with Mary, she is unfailingly indulgent of my need to understand. "I'll try to explain," she says after a session, "but understanding won't make any difference. The change has already *occurred* in your body." *Without my brain?* I never get over my discomfort with this idea.

*P*USHING HARD *against the wind, filling my chest with a child, the first hot shock of bathwater, a thumb running down my calf, soil rising between my toes, cold water on the back of my throat, the passing pleasure of evaporation, my son's hand before sleep, warm midwestern lake water, the liquid, tumbling drama of kissing.*

M*Y* LEFT LEG feels dead, unable to receive the energy I'm suddenly so good at whisking around my body at will. Mary begins a process of asking parts of my body to "speak." I'm on my back on the massage table. My upper arm rests on the table and my forearm is in the air. Mary takes my hand, lacing her fingers into mine, her fingertips relaxing against the palm of my hand. My fingers remain rigid and separate and straight.

"What does your hand want to do?" she asks.

I cannot explain why my hand remains stiff.

"How about, *Mary, I don't want this right now*," she says forcefully, at the same time causing my hand to cast hers away in a fluid gesture of defiance.

This rings like a bell through the great house of my body. Yet I cannot move.

Mary once again folds her hand into mine. "What does this hand want to do?" Again she flings her hand away, completing the motion my hand does indeed intend.

Finally, I repeat her words and the gesture. "Mary, I don't want this now." Something in me begins to crawl.

"Again."

"Mary, I don't want this now." Grit in it this time.

And when she folds her hand into mine the next time, my fingers close around hers with ease.

"You cannot say yes until you can say no," she says quietly. "That's what this hand knows."

This idea is not new, but the *experience* of the idea in my body is transformational. It *takes*.

R AIN SMELL ON WOOL; *curry, red as pollen; artichoke, clam, the tickle of salivation; tiles cool underfoot, fever's drenching sweat, thirst, cramp, itch, taste of blood.*

A LONG WITH OUR WORK on the physical plane, we enter the realm of image and visualization, which is more familiar to me from traditional therapy. Mary asks me to visualize aspects of myself as separate beings, to name those beings, and to call them up in interior dramas during which these silenced aspects can be expressed. I hate this exercise, too, and yet I begin to get information from it that surprises me. Most potent is the possibility that I have "abandoned," in Mary's words, an aspect of myself in the apartment bedroom.

The psychotherapeutic term *disassociation* describes this phenomenon, but it gives me no hint that I might "associate" again with the part of my consciousness that spent the night hovering near the ceiling. I've always described the effect of being raped as a loss, and Mary encourages me to view this expression as fact, not metaphor.

With Mary's prompting, I form an image of this disassociated consciousness as an individual, as someone I've left behind. As soon as I do this, I react with maternal energy. I want to get her out of there. I feel badly, as if I've literally left her trapped in the bloody chaos of that little room.

"Design her a new room," Mary advises. "But don't work on it, let it arise." And arise it does. The next time we meet, I close my eyes to a vision of a room of windows on three sides, high above the sea. The windows open outward like wings, like books. Below, the walls are indeed lined in bookshelves. The room is windy and white. On the tables are shells and rocks. Around the room are wooden easels, canvases blue, yellow, red. This is not the room I've built for my fear. A painter lives here.

THE CESSATION of thought, whispers across the collar-bone, flat swirl under an arm, smooth stones of bicep, breath in a shiver, tendons like arrows, the skin between the toes, pelvis liquid under a drumbeat, drawing in, breathing out, the slippage of reason.

I FIND MYSELF noticing bodies on the streets: one like a turtle carting around a heavy house, another just a sandwich board perched on the shoulders of a soul. My eating patterns and preferences change. Abruptly I want clothing that reveals. I lose fifteen pounds without effort. I start buying music and wean myself from all-news radio. I paint my office red.

After bodywork handed me a future, I felt a curious anger. Why hadn't I known about this sooner? The full impact of the hours that have passed in deprivation descends in the moment of relief. Rather than collapse, we muster indignation. Those who work with survivors are often the victims of such a backlash, abused themselves in this release of pent-up feeling and never adequately thanked or recognized for the lives they have saved.

I've come to believe that the body's memory is as deep and unacknowledged as our dreams. Both fall outside language, their messages carried in image and sensation. The training I needed to interpret these messages was available, but for a long time, it was invisible to me. Thankfully, among therapists who treat rape, incest, and battering survivors, bodywork is beginning to be seen as a companion to talk therapy. It's my hope that these techniques will be given a chance, not just by professionals but also by people like me, the wounded skeptics.

MY RELEASE comes too late to restore our marriage. On an October afternoon a few days before Halloween, Tim and I sit together in the house that was our refuge and tell Andre that we are getting a divorce. A cry flies out of him, and he arcs across our bodies to bury his head in the pillow. *You are going to change it,* he says through clenched teeth later that night when I put him to bed. *You will change it. You will, you will, you will.*

I don't have that much power, I tell him quietly, and though nothing is more true, I am never far from the leaden disappointment this failure brings. We have let him down. We can't fix it, can't give him what he wants, can't make the hurt go away. The next day, his favorite guinea pig dies just moments before Andre heads for the school bus, and I watch him retreat just as he was starting to bloom.

As I move through the legal process of divorce, soaked in grief, I am dimly aware of inhabiting myself. Later, I will realize that bodywork has actually changed me, restored my ability to touch and to be touched. Later, I will stop crying. I will learn to watch from the window as my son leaves my house to join his father for the week. I will learn to keep most of my heart with me when he goes, to wish them well, to look at Tim and see the father of my son, the friend of my youth, the man who gave me everything he could. I will learn to say, *Go, my beloved and be loved.*

Gretel, from a sudden clearing

No way back then, you remember, we decided,
but forward, deep into a wood

so darkly green, so deafening with birdsong
I stopped my ears.

And that high chime at night,
was it really the stars, or some music

running inside our heads like a dream?
I think we must have been very tired.

I think it must have been a bad broken-off
piece at the start that left us so hungry

we turned back to a path that was gone,
and lost each other, looking.

I called your name over and over again,
and still you did not come.

At night, I was afraid of the black dogs
and often I dreamed you next to me,

but even then, you were always turning
down the thick corridor of trees.

In daylight, every tree became you.
And pretending, I kissed my way through

the forest, until I stopped pretending
and stumbled, finally, here.

Here too, there are step-parents, and bread
rising, and so many other people

you may not find me at first. They speak
your name, when I speak it.

But I remember you before you became
a story. Sometimes, I feel a thorn in my foot

when there is no thorn. They tell me,
not unkindly, that I should imagine nothing here.

But I believe you are still alive.
I want to tell you about the size of the witch

and how beautiful she is. I want to tell you
the kitchen knives only look friendly,

they have a life of their own,
and that you shouldn't be sorry,

not for the bread we ate and thought
we wasted, not for turning back alone,

and that I remember how our shadows walked
always before us, and how that was a clue,

and how there are other clues
that seem like a dream but are not,

and that every day, I am less
and less afraid.

—MARIE HOWE

17

GIFTS

We can go without most things for long periods of time, anything almost, but not our joy, not those handmade red shoes.

—CLARISSA PINKOLA ESTÉS,
Women Who Run with the Wolves

OPENED UP by experience and disappointment, heroes in fairy tales learn how to recognize and make use of gifts. These stories argue that pain is a transformer, spinning straw into gold. Yet as a child, living in the realm of the concrete, I didn't always read the symbol for its truth. And so we may grow up unable to recognize a poison apple or a prince.

The stories of return are as important as the stories of descent. Some of what was stolen came back to me, but, as in a fairy tale, in an altered form. The transformation required love, patience, and the help of companions.

The Gift Re-created

THE GOLD BRACELET that I kept in Snowmaiden's box belonged, as I described earlier, to my grandfather, then to my aunt, and then to me. Its origins made it irreplaceable, or so I thought.

It came back at Christmas, nearly four years after the rape occurred and six years before Tim and I would separate. We drove with my sister Julie to the small town on the edge of Lake Michigan where my parents had recently settled. We'd never spent a Christmas with my parents before, nor were we to be together in that way again.

I remember the deep quiet and the fat lights on the forty-foot evergreen in the churchyard. I remember the snow, thick and animate, muffling the sounds of our tires on the still, old roads. It was a dreamlike seamless visit, sealed in my memory by images of plowing through the dark to a midnight service at the little frame church, tossing armloads of snow at one another on walks in the slow afternoons. I wore a plum-colored hat and coat that winter, and in the snapshots from that visit, I can see evidence of my happiness returning.

I think of that Christmas as the beginning of a rich and happy period in my life. Tim and I were married in the fullest sense. We had worked hard to repair the damage and were about to reach an island where we could rest. We knew it, and this sense of fruition was part of the joy of that Christmas. That we would not be traveling together to the end of our journey's road was knowledge hidden from us then.

My family believes in Christmas, in the potency of surprise, in the notion that an infusion of sparkle can help the spirit reach the spring. My mother still sends me wrapped trinkets, marked FROM: SANTA in my father's hand, to be slipped into my stocking on Christmas Eve. This particular Christmas, I recall feeling sleepy and satisfied and safe. With my loved ones close by, something frightened in me could relax.

When we'd finished opening presents that long, languid morning, as we began to stretch and clean up and think of food, Tim said: *There's one more present. It's for Pat, and it's not under the tree. It's on the tree.* Searching the branches, I found a white satin box with a gold beaded star on the lid. I was pleased at the idea of this and expected a token. Inside was my bracelet.

The sight of it, lying curled and golden in the little box, could not have been more shocking than if a living being had leapt into my hands. This was not the bracelet the rapist had stolen, but it looked *exactly like* that bracelet. For a moment, I believed it had been returned. The casual jangle of the bracelet on my wrist still brings back that flaring moment of hope resurrected. It is a powerful idea: forces operating without one's knowledge or participation can return the dead to life. What has been lost can be made to appear.

Later I learned the details—most acts of love being all about details. My mother still had her own bracelet from the set my grandfather had made for his daughters. Tim photographed it, and a master jeweler constructed a new bracelet from the photographs. The resemblance is exact, including the quirky seamless links, yet I regard it with greater care than I did the original. I no longer wear my wedding ring, but seven golden links remind me of how well loved I once was.

The Gift Transformed

My sister and I were born ten years apart. As adults, once again we came to live in the same city. When the decade turned for both of us, we resolved to spend our birthdays together. As the clock chimed thirty-forty, thirty-forty, we checked into our city's most appealing downtown hotel in the middle of a snowstorm and behaved like guests. Wandering that first afternoon, we were drawn to a shop of curious objects and to a small plate in the window of that shop. First in a series of limited editions featuring images drawn from Russian lacquer work, the plate held the image I'd lost a decade before: the Snowmaiden, exactly as I'd known her, the colors and details true, enlarged for this porcelain occasion.

The plate is considerably less beautiful than was the box, but the Snowmaiden is easier to see and the moon fully visible. Perhaps more important, the *story* of the Snowmaiden was unknown to me before I put my credit card down on that counter. A little pamphlet in translation told the story of Snegurochka, the Snowmaiden. I was comforted by its imagery, its accuracy. As the earth made its fortieth trip around the sun for me, I thought of Snegurochka's beautiful blue coat beginning to melt, her jewels turning to plain water, her safety as an innocent relinquished, her death just the other side of the music.

I'm glad she traded her safety for love and music, yet I understand her parents' dark warnings. When I look at her on my mantel now, I see the young woman I once was, who loved the sun in a cold climate, who heard powerful warnings and locked herself away from the music and the dancing. I see my mistakes, the harm to our marriage, and I know they demand of me forgiveness. When the flames have licked at your feet, it's natural to draw back from the fire. Sometimes we need a shepherd or a sister to help us leave a prison. The story is all there in the tilt of the Snowmaiden's head as she stands alone for the last time under the moon, a whisper of fear on the wind.

The Gift Translated

I'VE KNOWN JUDE since the first day we arrived at the University of Michigan and found that we liked just about everything better if we did it together. She stood with me the day I married Tim, kept track of the characters in my life stories, and can recall for me my own forgotten moments as the years have passed. She is the friend who accompanied me to Lake Harriet the day I saw the proportions of my fear.

That summer of our fortieth year, I traveled to Michigan to

celebrate her birthday. I gave her a token of love, a jeweled bee to wear at her neck, and she handed me a little box of power.

I don't remember ever mentioning to her the loss of the Russian lacquer box. I considered that a private grief, expected no one to understand how much I missed it—such a small thing. What I love best about the Russian lacquer box she gave me that year is that it does not carry the image of the Snowmaiden. This is the gift transformed. The image on this new box has sustained me throughout the writing of this book. It is always on the desk before me when I work. It is the image I hold to whenever I speak of what happened to me in the fourth decade of my life.

A circle of women dance around a blazing fire on the narrow oblong box. They are long haired and loose limbed, reminiscent of Matisse's huge women dancing in blue. But these women whirl in the night. Black sky, red flame, they hold one another's hands and circle the fire, the fire I lost for so long, the rollicking, binding energy of passion, the intensity of risk, the human bliss of sexual joy. Their dance became a conjecture, a possibility, a way to imagine a different kind of protection. Their presence stands for the strength there is in naked joy and the company of humans.

The Gift Let Go

My grandmother's watch was never found nor symbolically replaced. The watch I wear bears no relationship to what was taken from me, and I have lost so much time. I have lost *a time*. We can work toward transformation, and some of what we have lost will return. Some, we have to let go.

18

BEDTIME STORY/3

"THE SNOW QUEEN"

THE FOURTH PART

PRINCE AND PRINCESS

Gerda meets a sympathetic crow, someone who finally listens to her story. He speaks Crowtalk, which in Danish is the word for gibberish. He tells her a story about a prince he thinks is actually Kay.

"Do you know what *gibberish* means?" I ask, putting the book down and staring out the window. I am tired. It gets dark early now, and the windows are closed to the night air.

"Like you can't understand it," offers Andre with a quick shrug and the little hand motion I've come to delight in. This gesture paves the way for ideas about which he's unsure.

"Yes, and also things people think are helpful but turn out to be nonsense." I pause. "Like my idea about doing homework at a desk."

The crow tells Gerda the story of a princess who is terribly clever. When she decides to choose a husband, long lines of suitors arrive, but she finds none who can be at ease with her.

It was the third day, and there came a fellow with neither horse nor carriage who marched coolly up to the palace. His eyes were shining just like yours and he had lovely long hair, but his clothes were shabby.

Convinced that the boy who is now the prince is Kay, Gerda and the crow enlist the help of a palace crow to sneak Gerda inside. On the way to the bedchambers, she encounters swishing shadows on the wall.

They're only dreams! said the crow. They come and take their lordship's thoughts out hunting.

Gerda finds the prince and princess asleep in a room with a ceiling like a palm tree of glass leaves and two hanging beds shaped like lilies. She is disappointed to find that the prince is not Kay, but she lays down to sleep.

The dreams all came flying in again, and this time they looked like God's angels; they pulled a little toboggan behind them, and in it sat Kay nodding to her. But it was all nothing but a dream, and so it vanished as soon as she woke.

The next morning Gerda is provided with a golden carriage, a suit of new clothes, boots, and a muff. *The inside of the carriage was lined with sugared cakes, and on the seat were fruits and doughnuts.* The crow escorts her out of the kingdom, shedding tears as the carriage pulls away. *Aren't people kind—and animals, too, Gerda thinks.*

"Why is this taking so long?" Andre closes his eyes to stretch and yawn.

"Because it isn't easy."

"She shouldn't have gone to the palace, anyway. It was a waste."

"But she didn't know that. And she got a golden carriage and all those doughnuts. What would you say gave her the best clue about finding Kay in this part."

Andre doesn't hesitate to answer. "Her dream."

THE FIFTH PART

THE LITTLE ROBBER-GIRL

They drove through the dark forest, but the carriage shone like a flame. . . It's gold! It's gold! the robbers shouted, and, rushing out, they seized the horses, struck the little postilions, the coachman and the footman all dead, and then dragged little Gerda out of the carriage.

Andre listens carefully. What could be the explanation for his mother volunteering such a violent moment? How far would it go? Not as far as *Treasure Island,* he hoped. That was too far. That book, with its shiny cover full of beautiful pirates, still seemed to vibrate on the shelf across the room, like it was hot or alive. Would it go as far as the Merlin video she seemed to like? No, further—people had already been killed in this story. He glances at Sofi, who's sleeping over tonight, to see if she's listening for trouble.

Gerda is saved from death by a robber-girl who wants her as a playmate, though she threatens to kill Gerda if she does not behave. At the robbers' castle, which is full of ravens and bull-dogs and smoky fires, the robber-girl keeps a menagerie of animals that she mistreats. That night Gerda tells the robber-girl her story. Two ringdoves tell Gerda they have seen Kay flying in the Snow Queen's sled. They suggest she ask the reindeer how to find the Snow Queen's headquarters in Lapland. Gerda pleads with the robber-girl to oblige.

And she dragged a reindeer forward by the horn. . . . Every evening of his life, I tickle his neck with my sharp knife, and he's ever so frightened of it. . . . I always sleep with my knife! said the little robber-girl. You never know what may happen.

The robber-girl frees the reindeer under orders that he carry Gerda to the Snow Queen's summer palace. Before they leave, she provides Gerda with mittens, bread, and ham for the journey, but she keeps the muff given to Gerda by the princess.

There are my dear old Northern Lights! said the reindeer. Look at the way they're shining, and with that he ran even more swiftly, night and day. The loaves were eaten, and so was the ham, and then they found themselves in Lapland.

"Lapland?" Sofi giggles. "A land full of laps?

This makes her quite hysterical. "Exactly," I say calmly. Both she and Andre excel at astonishment bordering on outrage.

"Like everybody's running laps all the time," Andre throws in, ready to run off with the story.

"Like everybody's just a big lap," Sofi continues. "Just a big fat lap."

"I'd like that," I say. "If we were in Lapland, you could both fit on my lap." At this they wiggle closer, vying for space on my body. I hold them tightly, sobered, as they are not, by the robber-girl's casual cruelty and kindness.

19

JUSTICE

The events of our lives happen in a sequence of time,
but in their significance to ourselves, they find their own
order . . . the continuous thread of revelation.

—EUDORA WELTY

IN AUGUST 1991, just days before I began to write this
book, a man broke into a woman's apartment in the same neighborhood where a man had broken into my apartment a decade
before. He grabbed her by the hair, struck and choked her, raped
her. Though her screams alerted a neighbor to call 911 and though
the police arrived seconds after the man left the building, they made
no arrest. A year later, when a suspect in a series of rapes was finally
arrested, she joined thirteen others in bringing charges against
twenty-one-year-old Timothy Baugh and his nineteen-year-old
alleged accomplice, Shawn Enoch.

I attended portions of Baugh's trial in November and
December of 1994, drawn to it by the striking similarities
between reports of his crimes and my own experience. I nearly
didn't go. Thirteen years had passed for me, but time, as I'd
learned, is circular. I was afraid. I made up excuses. How would I
find the courtroom? How would I carve time out of my working

and parenting schedule to attend? How would I be able to sit in the same room with an accused rapist?

THIS WAS A CASE that nearly never came to trial—a series of unsolved rapes much like the rapes in my neighborhood a decade before. Five rapes with similar characteristics were reported between May and December of 1991. Similarities included an intruder who was self-assured and covered victims' faces during the rapes. Descriptions were given of a black male in his midtwenties with a round face and short stocky build.

Still, ten months had elapsed when the Minneapolis police released a sketch of the suspect and began to address a possible linkage among the rapes. Six more women were raped before the Minneapolis Bureau of Criminal Apprehension joined the case in December 1992, agreeing to supply four investigators to the Minneapolis Police Sex Crimes Unit. The last reported break-ins attributed to Baugh, one robbery and one rape and robbery, occurred in mid-December 1992. Three days later, the police finally established a thirteen-member task force to investigate what were now being called the crimes of a serial rapist.

On January 8, 1993, Timothy Baugh surrendered after being identified by his girlfriend and following intense negotiations between police and a local community activist who was a Baugh family friend. Out on bail for an unrelated charge, Baugh was already known to the probation system as a juvenile offender and burglar. He was charged with thirty counts of criminal sexual conduct, twenty-eight burglaries, twenty robberies, and three assaults, crimes that directly affected fourteen rape survivors and ten others. Shawn Enoch was charged with participating in six of the cases and arrested pending a separate trial.

• • •

TEN YEARS BEFORE, the series of rapes in this same neighborhood received barely a mention in the mainstream press. The *Minneapolis Tribune* had done an impressive three-part series on rape and its occurrence in Hennepin County that year, but no coverage was given to the rapes in my neighborhood. It's difficult to know how much of this was the result of survivors being reluctant to report the rapes and how much was under-reporting by the paper.

According to *Tribune* reports from the time, an average of two rapes a day were being reported in Minneapolis. If these had been murder statistics, perhaps they would have compelled coverage, alarm, the need for the newspaper to provide a community alert. I have since learned that a few homemade handbills were posted on trees to alert women in my neighborhood, but I hadn't seen them.

The rapes for which Timothy Baugh and Shawn Enoch were brought to trial eventually received prominent coverage in the *Star Tribune.* And with that coverage, what police might have dismissed as the work of a "professional" rapist became a high-profile case involving a "serial rapist." "Practically every stranger-type rapist is a 'serial rapist,'" said Lieutenant Robert Collins, chief of the Minneapolis Sex Crimes Unit, in a *Star Tribune* interview about media coverage of the case. "Rarely does a man go out and commit a rape successfully, then go home and say, 'That was nice; never again.' They usually keep going until they get caught."

Baugh's trial begins on October 20, 1994, but I am not there. I am across town teaching writing. I am following the news accounts, working up my nerve. On the third day of the trial, I make my way in the chilly rain to the Hennepin County Government Center in downtown Minneapolis, accompanied by a lawyer friend who offers to escort me into what feels like dangerous terrain. Jeanne and I take the elevators to the sixth floor, to the bland little court-room at the end of the hall, quiet and almost empty at 9 A.M.

The courtroom looks like a classroom, with several rows of theater seats for the jury on the left, the high judge's station, and a set of tables in an L shape on the right for the attorneys and defendant. The prosecution team sits with its back to the gallery, facing the judge and the table on which is piled a long row of physical evidence in grocery bags and manila envelopes, looking wrinkled and ordinary—clothes, a toy car, a keyboard, a phone answering machine.

Before the end of this day, the courtroom will be full, spectators overflowing into the hallway, but as the trial progresses, it is often nearly empty. I begin to feel like a regular. I often see the women of WATCH (Women at the Court House) with their red clipboards, volunteers who monitor the criminal justice system's handling of cases of violence against women in Hennepin County. Two other writers are in attendance, researching DNA evidence and writing a book on rape trials. There's a courtroom artist for a local television station, a man who keeps to himself and who I speculate is connected to one of the survivors, and a woman who sits in the back corner reading the paper and occasionally taking furious notes.

In the front row, Baugh's grandmother rests her head in her hands. She is here every day. Whenever I can, I sit at an angle from which I can watch her. The high cheekbones set in a round face testify to her relation to Baugh. Her steely hair is cropped close to her head like a man's, and she moves with a determined weariness.

For most of the trial, I believe this woman to be Baugh's mother until a press report identifies her as the grandmother who raised him. "She knows she raised him good, and she knows he's not the serial rapist," reports Baugh's cousin at the end of the trial. "There are many women in our family, and I feel if he had this thing for rape, he would have attacked one of his family members," she explains. When I read this I feel discouraged. The myth that rape is caused by some irrepressible sexuality persists, protecting us from the stark violence at rape's core.

A child of four or five squirms in the seat next to Baugh's grandmother. Eventually he falls asleep in the big chair. His face has a smooth sweetness that I recognize when Timothy Baugh enters the room.

ASSISTANT COUNTY ATTORNEY Anne Taylor blows past me with the forceful stride I come to love in her entrances and exits. A slight woman with straight brown hair that hangs long and loose down her back, she's always in a hurry, thrusting aside the swinging gate that separates the gallery, so its noisy banging announces her presence.

Throughout the trial, she maintains the barely restrained look of someone who has just argued with a spouse and is still so furious she can hardly be in the same room. Her lips slightly pursed, eyes refusing to light on anyone, she looks into the distance as if to avoid contact with the object of her fury. Her body language leads me to believe she *is* furious and struggling to contain her contempt for the man whom she is dedicated to putting away. I love her for this, and find her presence, her competence, and her comportment one of the most heartening aspects of this trial. The cavalry has arrived, and she is not fooling around.

The jury files in. Thirteen women and four men, fifteen white people, two black.

"All rise," calls the bailiff. And we do. As Judge Robert Lynn takes his seat on the high stage, I feel a thrill I don't expect. This is the thrill available to cynics, when something time-honored and suspect turns out to be moving. It occurs when we actively encounter a principle we have previously scorned as an abstraction. Trial by jury hasn't occupied my attention since high school civics, other than to malign it for its failure to protect women, people of color, political dissidents. Yet the idea in practice delivers a dramatic, nearly erotic charge.

My first glimpse of Timothy Baugh is a more potent moment than I have anticipated. This man did not rape me, but the instant he walks into the courtroom, I realize why I've come to witness his trial. The similarities between the reports of Baugh's crimes and the crimes committed against me make it easy to imagine a surrogate justice for myself.

I rarely think of the man who *did* rape me. Without an image by which to recall him, he has vanished from my fantasies. Sometimes I take comfort in an unfounded conviction that he has died as a consequence of drug abuse and crime, or that he's been imprisoned for some other offense. The possibility that he might be walking the streets of my town, in his early thirties by now, buying groceries and laughing at jokes, is not something I can allow myself to consider. But here, sitting before me, is someone who's been caught.

I hate Baugh the moment I lay eyes on him. As the trial progresses, I never grow tired of staring at him. I imagine I can project a hot needle of light, a force of concentrated disgust, across the room. I focus on his close-shaven head, his blank wide eyes. I imagine I can make his skin crawl. I never tire of the sight of the cops who accompany him to and from the courtroom to monitor his every move, their guns visible at their hips. I want to shout: *Look, Baugh, look over here! I'm free to come and go. I'm here to watch you suffer.*

I don't understand the hatred that motivates a rapist, but I sense I am close to it in my urge to see Baugh humiliated. I do not wish to *do* him harm, but I do wish him harm. I return to the notion again and again, touching it like a missing tooth, a sore place. It gives a kind of meaning to my day, a dark satisfaction. Apparently, when it comes to revenge, a surrogate will do very nicely. My desire to expel my pain *on the surrogate* is nearly automatic. From the moment Baugh enters in police custody, I recognize that no matter what the verdict, I will leave this trial comforted by Baugh's discomfort.

Even as I write these words, I hear them being spit back at me through clenched teeth. *I don't have any money,* he said. *There aren't any fucking jobs for someone like me. Did you go to college? Shut up. This is my job.*

"I have met no one who has seriously hurt someone that I could not document had been physically tortured as a child," said Hennepin County judge Isabel Gomez in an interview about young criminals. Some research indicates that 30 to 50 percent of men in prison for rape were sexually abused as children.

Whatever the root cause, I do not forgive Baugh or the man who raped me *anything* in these moments of identifying with vengeance. We are beings of will. We make choices. We do not always need to act out our desires—for pleasure or revenge. Nevertheless, I cannot escape the conclusion that the man who broke into my apartment did not act alone. He was accompanied by the demons who'd sunk teeth into his life years before, who'd deluded him into committing a crime that felt like revenge, and whom he fed with his narcissism, his ignorance, and his desperation.

T HREE DAYS OF TESTIMONY have already been given. Newspaper accounts fill me in on the opening statements and summarize the story of the first survivor to testify, the woman referred to as "the last victim." Her detailed and dramatic testimony provides an important piece of physical evidence against Baugh.

Just eighteen in December 1992, she lived with a roommate in an apartment in a placid area between two of our most beautiful city lakes. In one of the cold, glittery weeks before Christmas, when Minnesotans are beginning to huddle indoors, someone entered her basement apartment at two-thirty in the morning through a window left slightly open to moderate the effect of heating pipes running overhead.

The man demanded their video camcorder, something the woman and her roommate did not own. This led her to believe that the man had been watching them, since they had borrowed a camcorder the week before.

When I see this testimony in the newspaper, I remember Dorothy's certainty that my building had been watched and the break-in planned. It was no coincidence, she insisted, that the rape occurred when Tim and my sister both had left. I have always resisted this idea, as if the possibility itself could upset a delicate balance in my peace of mind.

The man called them liars when they denied having a camcorder. He said he hated liars. He threatened to blow their brains out with the gun he brandished. "He put the gun in our stomachs or our thighs and whispered 'bang,' as if he were imagining what it would be like to shoot us. He asked us if we liked it or if it felt good," the woman later told a reporter.

As the man prepared to rape her roommate, she remembered a long-past conversation. Her roommate had been speculating, as women often do, about how she might feel in exactly this situation. She had declared that she would ask the rapist to kill her—or would kill herself—rather than endure rape. The woman told the rapist not to hurt her roommate. He obliged. "Your friend is going to take it for you," he told her.

The roommate watched as he dropped to his ankles a pair of ripped stonewashed jeans and mustard yellow boxer shorts. Jeans and boxer shorts matching her description were later found in Timothy Baugh's apartment. The cash card he stole from these women was used that night by Baugh's girlfriend, Corina Laramee, whose photograph at the cash machine eventually led police to Baugh.

Both women identified Baugh in court, though they did not pick him out earlier from a group of photographs. During cross-examination, defense attorney Robert Miller began a line of questioning he would build throughout the trial, pressing the witnesses about what they *did not* notice that night: Baugh had a gold *T* imbedded in one of his front teeth.

Though I was not in the courtroom for this testimony, it received comparatively detailed coverage, including a follow-up interview with one of the witnesses after the trial. Following the attack she quit school, entered therapy, took more than seven self-defense courses. "When a friend insisted she had a right to walk through a park alone at night, she told her, 'It's not realistic anymore.'"

I am drawn to this woman and her story. I understand how the acknowledgment of danger can look more like fear than it actually is, how a sense of reality can't be altered by self-defense courses. I envy her remarkable bravery on behalf of her roommate. I am saddened by her roommate's conviction that rape would be "a fate worse than death" (a phrase that is listed as a synonym for *rape* in *Roget's Thesaurus*). I am curious about whether her roommate now believes, as I do, that life always contains possibilities, including the possibility of happiness for the rape survivor

THE FIRST TESTIMONY I actually witness comes from a man I'll call Robert, whose wife identified Baugh in court the day before as the man who broke into their apartment while they were watching television. They were robbed, but neither was sexually assaulted. Later, we hear her voice, cheerful and mechanical, on their answering machine, stolen that night and recovered from Baugh's apartment.

Robert talks of finding his watch among the property confiscated from Baugh's apartment. "I knew it was my watch," he explains with animation, "because of the masking tape on the band which always irritated my wrist."

I have imagined this same happiness about the triumph of the definitive detail. I have anticipated this momentary return of congruence when the police find my watch (with cleaning date recently engraved!), the Russian lacquer box (with its distinctive image of the Snowmaiden!), my gold bracelet (no seams!). Throughout the trial, I will experience a diffused solace from such points of identification with witnesses. In a sense, the trial is performing the function of theater for me. The structured telling of these stories enables an imaginative transaction that is deeply emotional and personal.

WHEN ASKED whether he saw posters or news reports about the serial rapes, Robert says, "I remember seeing a news report and not paying much attention to it." Every other man whom I hear testify offers a version of this response.

The women in my circle of acquaintances were on high alert during this period, watching the news and reading the paper for information about the most vulnerable areas of the city, the means of entry, the description of the rapist. I knew single women who had bars installed on basement windows, women who could not sleep during this entire period.

I took to calling other women to "talk me through" any late-night return to my darkened house. As soon as I'd step in the door, I'd have the portable phone in my hand and would tour the house, turning on lights and looking in closets, accompanied each step of the way by the voice on the other end of the line.

• • •

At the morning break, my friend returns to work, and I strike up a conversation with a middle-aged woman in the gallery. She looks a bit out of place, and she's eager to talk. She tells me that she survived one of the three St. Paul rapes linked to Baugh that will be tried in the Ramsey County court system.

She says it's hard to hear the case under discussion today referred to as the last attack. "It wasn't the last one," she whispers, intent on getting this across, even though the jury has returned, and it's time to start again. "He broke into my house five days later. My seven-year-old was there when he raped me." Her eyes are opaque with the uselessness of her pain; it disorients, distracts. I want to tell her it will be better soon, but I'm not sure that's true. I cover her hand with mine. She tells me that she's going to attend every single day, but I never see her again.

Yesterday the prosecution's star witness caused a stir by failing to show up. Rumor has it that she will testify today. By the time Baugh's former girlfriend testifies, the courtroom is overflowing. The heavy door opens and closes as men in suits with laptop computers, agitated reporters, and slightly desperate onlookers scan for a seat and are forced to leave.

The courtroom feels sexually charged, and because this is my first day at the trial, I make the mistake of thinking it will always affect me this way. Awareness literally overpowers the room. It's like being in a pickup bar or stranded in an elevator; there's a sense that we may play a role in one another's destiny. Though there aren't any cameras, we regard one another with photographic intensity. *Who are you? Where do you stand? Why are you here?* I look at the jury and find myself thinking: How does anyone play *that* role when behind our righteousness lie so many mistakes, such human frailties?

Baugh's grandmother has been joined by the family friend who negotiated Baugh's surrender to police, three young women who could be sisters or cousins, and a young man draped in gold rings and chains. The racial division in this courtroom is dramatic. All of the survivors are white. The lawyers, the judge, and most of the jury are white. Both of the accused are black. What must it be like for the jurors to look out on this white, white room and see just one row of black faces, all belonging to the supporters of the accused?

The race of the man who raped me rarely enters into my thinking. Although I never got a clear look at him, I surmised from his voice and a flash of vision before I was blindfolded that he was black. It has mattered very little. For a while I was more wary than usual around black males I did not know, but I have always carried that wariness, relatively unexamined from childhood, like a bad habit.

Statistics consistently refute the mythology about black-on-white rape. In fact, same-race rape is the norm, and white men make up the majority of men arrested for rape. It causes me to wonder about the sociological factors that may be at work in the neighborhood where all these rapes took place. Researchers working anthropologically have found that violence in young males across societal groups seems to be related to access to status. I find it notable that these rapes took place in an inner-city crossroads where the transient, the poor, the middle class, and the rich pass one another every day.

O N THE WITNESS STAND, Corina Francis Laramee swivels in her chair, boldly casual, yanking it back and forth with the force of her torso as she waits for the proceedings to proceed. She has the high good spirits of someone who has always known she was destined for attention.

In her responses to Anne Taylor's opening questions, we learn that Laramee has four children and that the oldest is twelve. Laramee is twenty-five. I lose my moorings and the slight disdain I've been feeling toward her—*girlfriend of the accused, didn't show up to testify.* I calculate: she gave birth at thirteen, and at fifteen, seventeen, twenty-one. I lean forward in my chair, prepared to listen differently from the way I was a moment before. *Thirteen, fifteen, seventeen, twenty-one.* Later Laramee testifies that she has known Baugh for six years, though he is not the father of any of her children. They had lived together on and off for six months at the time of his arrest, and she tells us that she still cares for him.

She tells of being awakened at 2:30 A.M. by the light in the bedroom.

"And what did you see?" asks Taylor.

"Tim," Laramee answers, and he suddenly becomes ordinary, somebody's brother, somebody's neighbor. "He asked me, did I want to go to the cash machine? First I said no, and then I said, yeah."

"Did he *have* a cash card?" probes Taylor.

"No," Laramee explains. "He told me he got it out of the trunk of a car."

In her presence, such a story seems easy to swallow. With Christmas coming on, you might not question the boyfriend who brings in the money to support your four children. Perhaps you wouldn't ask too many questions; wouldn't try to imagine where he got the pin number. Perhaps you'd rise in the middle of the night and do your part, go down the street to the cash machine and get fifty bucks.

When I locate crime *out there,* it seems inevitable or unlikely or the fate and fault of people far different from myself. Listening to Corina, I can imagine the brittle mid-December air and the slumbering residential streets she crossed to help her boyfriend. Fifty bucks—no big deal to *them*, whoever they are.

The police arrived at Laramee's apartment on January 5 to take her downtown to answer questions. They asked if she knew anything about a serial rapist, and she said no. Up until this point, she claims she thought Baugh's criminal activities were limited to robbery. She admits that she told police a lie about getting the cash card from two men named Steve and Paul, then laughs at herself because the police do not buy her flimsy story. In this moment I see her, perhaps in high school, confessing some fabrication to her girlfriends, and as she does so, she is a bit charmed by her own boldness, her inventiveness.

Once she's in the police car, she learns that she's being charged as an accessory to rape.

"How can I be an accessory to rape?" she protests. "I don't have a penis."

This provokes the only courtroom laughter I witness in the six-week trial. Everyone laughs. I love this moment of release, grateful to share something other than horror with the people in this little room. I forget to look over at Baugh.

W HEN WE BREAK for lunch, an unlikely group gathers by a bank of elevators that prove to be criminally slow. Corina and her youngest child stand alone, without the protective escort accorded other witnesses. Her daughter wears pink barrettes in her hair and twists her toe on the carpet in boredom. Baugh's grandmother stands with her feet planted slightly apart, moving her dentures around in her mouth, avoiding Corina, staring at the floor and then up at the lighted numbers over the elevator.

Robert Miller strides up, his hair brushing the collar of his *Miami Vice* suit. His assistant, a red-haired woman who looks like she could work in a hip record store, speaks briefly to Baugh's grandmother. Miller ignores Corina, who busies herself with her child just a few steps away. Several members of the jury wait awkwardly next to me.

I wonder how we can all be standing here together like the equals we are not inside the courtroom. There's nothing to do, nothing to say. We are all hungry. We all want out. Prosecutor Anne Taylor arrives just as the elevator doors open. Loaded down with file folders, she appears to be working through lunch. I want to speak to her, but we descend in total silence. I feel like a fan, thrilled to be riding with the stars of the show.

Downstairs, the press is waiting for Corina. Men with heavy cameras on their shoulders jounce after her across the slick floors of the Hennepin County Government Center as she dashes around a corner to the escalator. It's disheartening to watch grown men chase her. This is a woman who would attract no attention for anything else she has ever done. Yet I am drawn to the spectacle myself—want to watch them watch her, unable to ignore the command of the amplified moment.

THE FOLLOWING MONDAY testimony resumes, but I can't attend any sessions during this third and most interesting week. Eight women capable of sitting in the presence of the man whom they believe raped them will testify. Their stories are summarized in *Star Tribune* reporter Margaret Zack's daily coverage. I try to read between the lines of the clippings that Jeanne sends me throughout the trial, aware that for me there is no substitute for being in the courtroom.

I am seeking something particular from these proceedings that I can't get secondhand. Occasionally, a line that Zack writes strikes a chord. *Most of the victims have said they never spent another night in their apartments.* At the edge of the facts, which don't belong to me, are truths that validate, affirm, clarify, and include me. *How are people going to feel when they find me? I just honestly thought I was going to die, she said in pretrial testimony.* As the stories accumulate under headlines that diminish the lives they summarize, I find myself fighting despair, wanting to know these women, wanting not to know, not to do the numbers. These women plus me, multiplied by too many.

THE FIRST RAPE attributed to Baugh occurred on May 9, 1991, a few miles from my old apartment. A nineteen-year-old woman woke to a noise she thought was her kitten. "I opened my eyes and saw a figure come out of the closet. I saw a man standing in front of me with a gun."

Four months later, a twenty-four-year-old woman confronted two men outside her bedroom in an apartment close to the scene of the previous attack. She was told she'd be killed if she looked at them, and then, she testified, the shorter man called her a bitch and said he was going to get some.

At first, she refused to remove her clothes but complied after being hit and threatened with death. The newspaper account reports, "He kept talking to her, though she said the last thing she wanted to do was converse." *Yes,* I think, *truly the last, unless you count dying.*

The court also heard testimony from a woman who was raped ten days later, on September 17, 1991. Her roommates were not raped. One was tied up but not assaulted, and the second never left her bedroom. This witness was ordered to lie on her back on the porch floor, and a chair cover was placed over her head. She was raped by two men, and afterward the first asked her for a cigarette. This woman could not identify Baugh in line-ups or in court.

Her fear now is "kind of a constant thing," she said.

• • •

THE NEXT DAY, Zack reports the testimony of a woman who lived farther south, closer to the lakes in one of the most beautiful residential areas of the city. It was just a week before Christmas 1991. Twenty-three years old at the time, she was alone in her apartment reading in bed when a man ran into the bedroom, jumped on her, and covered her head with a pillow.

"When he asked her how long she'd lived in the apartment and whether she'd lived abroad, she became angry. 'I sat up and said he had to leave or at least let me get dressed,' she testified." He called her sassy, said she "deserved it," and then raped her and choked her into unconsciousness.

Three months passed. A twenty-three-year-old woman and her roommate found an intruder in their apartment when they returned from having coffee at 5:30 A.M. Later, I am in court when the intake nurse testifies about this woman's hospital examination. The nurse reports that the young woman's legs and fists remained clenched throughout the pelvic examination. I suddenly ache for this woman I'll never meet. I know how the body can freeze at the point of trauma, a kind of witness, offering evidence in its own language. (When I read testimony from the William Kennedy Smith trial, I am struck by the nurse's description of Patricia Bowman in the hospital as "regressed, curled up on the stretcher.")

"During the attack, the seventh survivor asked her assailant: 'Don't you have a mother, a sister? What would you do if this happened to them?' He said, 'I'd kill him.'"

I RETURN TO COURT on November 9, the third week of the trial. Baugh's grandmother is in court alone today, sitting in the same spot. I stare at her hands, large as a man's, cradling her chin. The morning begins with testimony by a nurse-clinician from the Sexual Assault Resource Center, the agency that staffs the Rape Center at Hennepin County Medical Center. Her testimony concerns the final witness from the previous week.

This woman, the oldest survivor, was accosted on March 28, 1992, at six-thirty in the morning in the parking lot of her apartment building. I've read of her testimony in the newspaper, but today her name appears on a poster carefully lettered in black and white in the front of the courtroom. On an easel like the one my son uses for watercolor painting are color snapshots of her wrecked apartment arranged and labeled like a school project—a visual aid illustrating breeds of horses or the Greek islands. The photos of her apartment recall for me the way our bedroom looked when Tim and I returned to it together. I picture the wooden lamp that Tim made from a kit, broken yet still hanging lopsided like an injured thing.

Prompted by Taylor, the nurse is asked to draw the woman's injuries on a life-size chart of the body. "Photographs were taken," she says. After verifying the Polaroid photos, the nurse cites multiple bruises, bruises on the face and on areas of the body that had been bound by the telephone cords. The silence in the courtroom as she draws these wounds with Magic Marker is total, as if we've all stopped breathing. I suddenly want to see the photographs taken of *my* injuries, want to look at myself from the distance of the future, notice what happened to my body, show others, remember.

The nurse testifies about the evidence she gathered: a slide of sperm fluid, hair samples. She testifies about labeling the evidence and putting it in a locked refrigerator. On cross-examination, Miller quizzes her closely about where, how, and when she collected the evidence. "Do you *believe* or do you *know*?" he probes in response to an answer about sealing the evidence.

I am in this moment relieved of the sense of violation I felt in the examining room at Hennepin County Medical Center. At the time, I wanted comfort. I wanted to be left alone. I struggled with the fact that I was being commanded to follow someone else's agenda. But here, as I watch Anne Taylor build her case, as police officers, nurses, shoe print experts, DNA experts, all testify, I understand that justice can hinge on the responsible actions of strangers. I am grateful for the careful work of these people whose jobs are both routine and momentous.

Four names are displayed on the poster boards after lunch. For some reason these names are familiar, as if I've dreamed them, so it does not surprise me when I leave changed by the testimonies of the two young men who take the stand next.

The man I'll call James Sanderson is at ease as he crosses to the witness stand. Dressed in a leather jacket, his long hair pulled back in a bushy blond ponytail, his manner is casual, as if his appearance here is entertaining to him or at least interesting. His demeanor is in marked contrast to the women and the expert witnesses whose testimonies I have seen, who all seem oppressed by their knowledge.

His former roommate, a man I'll call Adam Brown, will testify the following day, giving his own version of the events he and Sanderson experienced with the two women who will also testify. I've combined their testimonies here, but want to note that Brown is a small, wiry man who also displays a calm, appealing confidence.

Sanderson tells the story easily. He and Brown lived in an apartment on the edge of Uptown, the neighborhood full of rental units where most of the rapes took place. On June 13, 1992, a woman friend from out of town was visiting. At ten-forty-five on that summer evening, she and Sanderson were sitting on the couch in the living room when they saw the woman who lived upstairs cross in front of the window with a man Sanderson did not know. Moments later, the door to their apartment opened, and the man entered, holding the woman in a headlock with a gun to her head. He quickly assessed the situation and ordered Sanderson and his friend to lie down on the floor.

It is here that Sanderson's testimony delivers its first shock. "He does not force me to lay down and so I do not," Sanderson explains calmly. "I crouch."

"He asks me for my purse," Sanderson continues, noting the man's reference to his long hair. Brown, meanwhile, was on the telephone in a back room of the apartment. Hearing noises he could not place, he put the telephone down without hanging it up and acting on a hunch, retrieved his field hockey stick from the back bedroom before walking into the living room. Meanwhile, the man had shut the drapes and picked up the phone after hearing a voice on the other end calling for Adam.

"Who's Adam?" he asked.

"I am," said Brown, emerging from the back room. The man ordered Brown to drop the hockey stick, which he did not do, and to tell the person on the phone to remain on the line. Brown got down on the floor with the stick beside him as the man demanded money and cash cards, repeatedly threatening to kill them.

STOP RIGHT HERE, I want to say. The words suddenly seem incapable of conveying anything of significance. I have been through this and even I can let these stories roll past me with a nod: *Yes, repeated threats that he would kill them, yes, and so what happened next?* It becomes a story, a TV movie of the week, so quickly.

I am conscious, too, of telling *you* a story, without enough pauses for imagination to place you in these apartments in the middle of the night, in these young lives, awakened from common dreams and asked to accept the end of dreaming, in time slowed way down while the rights you've been taught were granted at birth are revoked for no reason you will ever be able to grasp.

How were you feeling?" prosecutor Taylor asks Sanderson.

"Upset, appalled, waiting for an opportunity to stop him. I felt he was overly confident, not expecting any resistance. He'd made mistakes, and I felt he would make more. He didn't force me to lie all the way down. He let Adam lie down next to the field hockey stick. He didn't hang up the phone."

These words become for me some of the most startling testimony in the entire trial. I recognize in them an attitude fundamentally different from my own. James Sanderson did not react to this intruder only with panic and terror. The path his mind took in a crisis *assumed* power, *assumed* an ability to overpower, *assumed* action. How different this was from my sense of my own choices—to acquiesce, to appease.

I don't want to imply a judgment about the choices made by any victim or survivor, including me. I did what I believed I could, what I sensed was right, but I felt envy as I listened to this young man. I envied him his default setting, his ability to resist, an ability that was partly a function of his training. And this gave me hope, a desire to borrow what is powerful about masculine socialization: the orientation toward problem solving, the emphasis on action, the use of a focused and harnessed anger to refuse mistreatment.

At a certain point, Sanderson saw his opportunity and stood up, a choice made easier by the fact that he had never fully lain down. He screamed, then ordered the man to drop his gun. The intruder lunged. "I had the impression I was going to be kicked," Sanderson said and grabbed for the man's right leg, throwing him onto the couch. By this time, Brown was on his feet and hit the intruder in the back of the head with the hockey stick. The man spun and shoved Brown against the wall, after which a fight broke out.

"I remember particular moments," says Sanderson. "I think I hit him in the face. I remember a chair in the air." Brown recalls the chair hitting him, the mirror behind the couch breaking, and all three of them crashing into it. He recalls hitting the man from the front with the hockey stick held horizontally and believes this is when the gun was dropped.

At some point after the gun was dropped, the two women opened the apartment door, which led into the hallway. According to Brown, one crouched down and held the door open while hiding behind it. The other woman and the intruder ran out, followed by Brown, and they all crashed into the landing. Brown used the butt of the hockey stick to hit the man again, chasing him out onto the sidewalk until he saw him turn the corner. He recalls his hands slick with blood, unable to grip the stick. I am startled when he estimates that the whole incident took just five to seven minutes.

Inside, James Sanderson called 911. We hear the 911 tape, and it provides a glimpse of the terror missing in these calm, structured testimonies. As in the O. J. Simpson trial, the raw heart of the crime is easily lost in the careful legal accountings that make up the trial. In this case, we are given a sense of that remarkable first moment on the other side of disaster, when the world is blessed and unfamiliar, when you struggle to accept your aliveness and already know it will never be yours again in quite the same way.

Sanderson remains on the stand as we listen to the tape, and it's hard to reconcile his composure with the disarray we sense from his voice on the tape. We hear startlingly heavy breathing that goes on and on and does not stop. He gasps and gulps air. He simply cannot catch his breath. He delivers the necessary information clearly, and then there is silence when the operator is off the line, checking something. We hear Sanderson talking to himself in possibly the first full moment he's had to reflect. "I can't believe I had the courage to do that," he says quietly to himself.

Suddenly I want this grace and strength for my son, this beautifully masculine combination of gentleness and competence and determination. I am briefly in love with these two men, gazing after them as they leave the courtroom, wishing them well.

THE LAST TESTIMONY of the afternoon throws me so completely that I am unable to return to the trial for another week.

A circle of seven women and a single man enclose the woman who will testify as she waits in the glassed-in corridor outside the courtroom. They scrutinize everyone who enters and leaves. I feel a certain obligation to function as a reporter, to linger in the hallway and stare. I don't have the heart for it. I head for the bathroom, though I have nothing to do there. I pat my hair, notice the sadness in my face.

An impression has solidified in the hallway, an impression that remains with me long after the trial has ended. There are women visible everywhere in this trial: the prosecutor, the defense assistant, the court reporter, most of the jury, many of the nurses, cops, and detectives who testify, the witnesses and the advocates who accompany them, female reporters and writers, and the women of WATCH. Just as I feel concerned about the lack of black faces in this courtroom, I am heartened by the number of female faces. It helps counter the fact that women face an uphill battle for justice in rape trials.

• • •

Before the witness testifies, a nurse chronicles the woman's injuries: an inch-long laceration in her vagina, skin torn around her anus, a laceration on the wall of the anus. She bled so much, the witness later testifies, that the rapists had to stop during the assaults to wipe up the blood.

Baugh does not look at her as she takes the stand. He appears to be reading notes on a legal pad, physically moving his head across the page. Robert Miller chews on a pink pen. The woman holds herself stiffly, as if to keep a fragile unity from shattering. I am worried about her. Presumably, the last time she and Timothy Baugh were in a room together, she was unable to believe that the world was safe, comprehensible, predictable. She keeps her head down. I'm reminded of my own desire for invisibility that morning when I left my apartment.

Baugh lifts his head and watches as Anne Taylor goes over the layout of the witness's apartment on a chart. She draws in furniture on the blank layout sketch. The woman answers the routine questions in a terribly quiet voice. Baugh resumes reading. She has not looked at him.

She begins to tell her story, prompted by Taylor's sensitive questioning. On the night of October 16, 1992, she'd been downtown listening to music until 11:20 P.M. "I came inside and went to sleep," she says, her voice barely audible. Already it looks as if this is too hard for her. She has entered the memories that threaten equilibrium.

"Do you recall if the blinds were down?" asks Taylor.

"I have a cat and I leave them up. One light was on." Tears, trembling. She is having trouble speaking. There are long pauses between her phrases. "I was completely asleep. They are coming at me, and I don't know who you are. *Quit screaming or I'll kill you*, the short one says. *I have a knife and I'll slit your throat.* Who could be in my room? They are very close. Right here."

She has switched midsentence and with chilling ease into the present tense, a startling demonstration of how post-traumatic stress compels us not to recall but to relive. What will happen here?

Taylor brings her back to the narrative. I try to follow her story. The two men turn on the light, tell her to turn over in bed, not to look at them. The taller one throws the bedcovers off onto the floor. "They are kind of walking around the room. *Shut up— just shut up.* One would ask questions and the other would say shut up."

They force her to kneel on the floor while they ransack the room, handling her jewelry. "The taller one asks where my money is." She tells him about the seven dollars in the pocket of her jacket. "The short one said, *Spread your cheeks.* I wouldn't." She's crying, can hardly get the words out. "It hurt. He pushed me into the bed and raped me rectally. The other guy is screaming: *What's your pin number?* It's so hard to remember your pin number when it's hurting so much."

THE COURTROOM is totally silent. Her story comes out in bursts of present-tense action, interrupted by shaking tears. She looks thin and young and not up to this.

"The taller man said, *She's messing with us.* I looked around at him. *Quit looking at us or I'll kill you.* They tell me to get on the bed on my stomach. *I'm gonna get some,* the taller one says. Now I'm on my hands and knees. His knees against my knees, he rapes me vaginally. The short one says, *Back her up,* and he drags me backward. *You're gonna suck on me. Don't do anything stupid.* He has a gun to my head. *Suck on me like you do your white boyfriend. If you let me go limp, I'll kill you.* Then he told me to arch my back and raped me vaginally. *Quit crying.* They throw covers over me. Running around opening drawers."

Miller seems in pain. Baugh is expressionless. I have essentially left the room. I hear the rest of her testimony, but I am unable to corral my spirit. It wants to go. Every time I return to this woman's story, as I transcribe my notes, write this account, review it, and rewrite it, trying to treat it like material to be shaped, I meet the despair I succumbed to in the courtroom. Whatever the witness was actually feeling, I saw in her an utterly overwhelmed and disorganized spirit. Her story and her visible disruption were too much for me. Thirteen years have enabled me to restore my life, even to enlarge it, but I have been left vulnerable to fear and to anger and to despair. I have almost no ability to fight despair.

SHE TALKS ABOUT the strawberries. When she walked into her kitchen after the men had finally left, she saw the green tops of the strawberries she'd had in the refrigerator littering the floor. She can't get over this detail. The fact that someone could eat strawberries after brutalizing another human being preoccupies her more than the story she has just remembered for us.

I can't get over the details either. I can deny an abstraction, but the details haunt me like the dead. As she describes the small insult of the strawberries, for a moment I picture them on the floor of *my* kitchen, the one I left behind that August morning. They are scattered across the odd confetti linoleum in that funky old place whose kitchen wallpaper was an orange and green wash of flowers, whose dark woodwork made the ragged oriental rug look fine, whose windows coaxed to life all those plants I had time for before I had a child.

"My cat was missing," she reports. "They said, *If you call the police, I'll kill you.* Which neighbor should I wake up?" she wonders out loud for us, dismissing one choice because, "I didn't want to say these things in front of her seven-year-old."

I'm on the edge of my seat. I want to go to her. I'm afraid for her. I am angry with her. I am furious that she's having such a hard time, doing so badly. I am a little sick from holding in so much feeling, quietly taking notes.

I look at Baugh, and he turns and looks right back at me. It's a strange moment. Satisfying and chilling. He's had to make a deliberate decision in order to look in my direction. I've been boring my hot gaze into him all these days in court. This is the first time he's looked back. He holds my eyes just a moment. I'm struck by the strangeness of us all being together in the same room.

AFTER SHE LEAVES the courtroom, her family and friends also leave, and the room feels empty. We who remain, the jury, the reporters, a few others in the gallery, are left with knowledge that seems too heavy for us. We need more people to carry this load; we cannot bear it alone. I cannot bear it.

I walk out into the gray falling night feeling as if I've lost my world all over again. I have trouble driving, am dead to the bleak November avenues, consumed by the hugeness of evil, how in its presence so little seems left that matters. When I arrive at my empty house alone (Andre is with his father this night) I do a strange thing. I call Tim.

We hardly speak these days except in our divorce mediation proceedings. Yet, in my deep sadness, he rises in my heart as the one person on earth with whom I can share this burden. I cry, talk with him about the sad world. I tell him about the woman who testified, about how fractured and fragile she seemed, yet there she was in the courtroom, confronting Baugh. I tell him about James Sanderson and Adam Brown, how I wanted to be like them, how I found hope in their attitudes and actions. And then I tell him, possibly for the first time, that I wish he had been home that August night. I tell him how much I had needed him, how I regretted that we did not go through that night together. "You can always call," he tells me, his voice kind and steeped in our sadness. "Call again tonight if you need to." I cry hard and sleep well, dreaming of the men in my life.

THE NEXT WEEK is taken up with testimony from prosecution witnesses about the DNA evidence against Baugh. In January, Judge Robert Lynn had ruled that certain aspects of DNA evidence would not be admissible in this trial, based primarily on a 1989 Minnesota Supreme Court ruling. That ruling made Minnesota one of only two states to limit the admissibility of DNA evidence. Specifically, the prosecution could not enter into evidence the fact that there was a statistical probability of only one in eighty-nine million that someone other than Baugh committed these rapes.

At that point, ten months before the trial took place, Anne Taylor took an unusual step. In an effort to persuade Lynn to reconsider his ruling, two survivors testified privately before Judge Lynn, emphasizing the fact that they had been unable to see their attackers. Lynn reversed his ruling, and in April, the Minnesota Supreme Court revisited its decision, widening the use of DNA evidence in Minnesota trials.

This was crucial for the prosecution because, before the trial, only one of the thirteen women Baugh is alleged to have raped had positively identified him. "In most of these cases, the victims' heads were covered," said Minneapolis Police Sergeant Nancy Olson, who headed a task force in the Baugh case. "They couldn't make any identifications. There weren't any prints. There was nothing else except for DNA."

· · ·

On the first day of defense testimony, the Baugh family row is full. Baugh is dressed in an Easter-egg blue suit. He enters the courtroom smiling, nearly swaggering. I see his gold tooth. He doodles with a black pen, looks like a kid who wouldn't meet his mother's eye. I'm sitting next to the TV artist. The reporters discuss the relative merits of duck and goose for Thanksgiving dinner. Baugh appears oblivious, but watching him closely, I see he is acutely aware of all comings and goings.

Miller seems to enjoy his moment on the offense, infusing his questions with the implication that he's got an ace up his sleeve: he's uncovered foul play. A fingerprint expert testifies that it would be unusual for someone to touch nearly seventy different items and leave no prints. No identifiable fingerprints were found in any of the Minneapolis cases, and none of the survivors remember that Baugh was wearing gloves.

Miller challenges the ability of any witness to identify Baugh, emphasizing the dark rooms, the fact that faces were covered. He casts suspicion on the long pauses in deposition tapes, suggesting that witnesses were being coached by police during these pauses.

Baugh's grandmother leaves the courtroom, her chronic cough overcoming her. The last witness to testify this first day is Baugh's aunt, a woman barely older than Baugh. She tells the story of Baugh trying to get food out of a skillet as a five-year-old and spilling hot liquid on his stomach. None of the survivors mentioned the resulting scar in their descriptions of the rapist. The family laughs at her delivery. She is calling up an old story. I wonder what actually happened, about the harshness of Baugh's childhood.

Baugh and Miller confer. Baugh has a dazzling smile, an animated face that might charm a relative or girlfriend. I'm struck by all the effort here to prove *if*, and how little we will understand when it's over about *why*.

• • •

THERE ISN'T ANY CONSENSUS about the constellation of factors which "cause" or at least permit rape. Some research supports the argument for biological drivers of male sexual violence. Because primitive men had to fight for sexual access, this theory asserts, there has been a resulting natural selection for sexual violence. Additionally, men produce ten times more testosterone than women, a hormone that predicts an attitude that has been described as "me first." Testosterone prepares humans to fight for what they want. Both power and sexual interest have been shown to drive the testosterone surges in men.

On the other hand, anthropologists have found social structures radically different from the American model that also produce a radical decrease in rape. Cultural anthropologist Peggy Reeves Sanday studied ninety-five modern band and tribal societies and found 45 percent to be virtually "rape free." The United States has the highest incidence of rape of any society in the world by a staggering margin. A woman is thirty times more likely to be raped in the United States than in Japan, eighteen times more likely than in Great Britain.

Sanday's research leads her to assert that "human sexual behavior cannot be divorced from the larger system of beliefs, values, and attitudes." In *A Woman Scorned*, Sanday looks at the effect that American "sexual culture" may have had on jurors in the recent acquaintance-rape trials of William Kennedy Smith, Mike Tyson, and others.

It is difficult not to sink under the weight of such information. As a survivor, I am in this courtroom hoping for justice, but as a human being I am hungry for understanding. Rape remains one of the most intractable mysteries of human behavior, so complex it has thus far defied explanation and treatment. My hopes at this stage are simple: we will make it a point of pride to raise sons who respect the integrity of women's lives, and daughters who know how to use the power of the truth.

I AM IN MY KITCHEN. I hear the news on public radio. After twenty hours of deliberation, the jury has convicted Timothy Baugh on all eighty-three counts. I have a dishtowel in my hands and my mind is on my sister's birthday, but the news floods me with light. Later that night, a local television station interrupts a prime-time telecast of the cartoon *Frosty the Snowman* for a bulletin about Baugh's conviction, setting off a storm of protest from parents.

Baugh is given the longest sentence ever handed down in Minnesota—139 ²/₃ years. He will not be eligible for parole for ninety-three years. Judge Lynn's words are swift and satisfying. "Your right to live among free people has been forfeited. My intent is for you to spend the rest of your life in prison."

Baugh's grandmother is not in the courtroom.

But six of the survivors are there to address the court with victim-impact statements, a right granted in Minnesota only since 1988. Each is allowed to tell the court how the crime affected her, to tell in her own words of the damage done.

"Timmy wanted to leave," defense attorney Robert Miller told the *Star Tribune*. "I'm paraphrasing what he said, but it was something like, *I don't have to sit and listen to this, do I?*"

Shawn Enoch is later convicted of eight counts of rape and twenty-three counts of robbery and burglary in a separate trial. Enoch's mother asks the judge to have mercy on her son, saying he was fathered by a man who raped her.

WHEN I WATCH the city recycling truck roll down the street, I remember when I first heard the word *recycling* thirty years ago, in college, in Ann Arbor, Michigan. It was an eccentric gesture performed by my most radical friends. It marked them as quaint and principled, like the Amish.

There was no speculation then about whether this behavior would have an impact on the world. The glass and tin that could be saved by a few passionate oddballs was symbolically admirable, but symbolism was a weak thing, I thought at twenty-one, when compared to mountains of garbage. I marched against the Vietnam War anyway, but in my private heart, I was skeptical about whether our shouts would carry beyond our own crowd.

Now, each Monday when the recycling truck stops at *each house* on my block, its back brimming with tin and glass, I have to acknowledge the power of symbol. The facts of my life include the fact that individuals working in small, unnoticed ways can change the world.

And sitting in the courtroom, I again felt the icy edge of that old heart fall away as I watched Anne Taylor at work, as I watched the survivors testify, as I watched a courtroom remain respectful, as I watched a judge turn in a sentence unmistakable in its severity.

Fifteen years ago when I was raped, the law giving victims the right to speak in court did not exist in Minnesota. Fifteen years ago, the phrase heard most commonly about a rape trial was that it was a *second rape.* Certainly the justice system continues to disappoint rape survivors. But all over my town, this trial and this verdict were seen as signs of change.

From "The Veils"

We are born in cauls and veils, and our lives as women are fierce and individual dances of shedding them. We are stepping higher, higher now, into the thinnest air. It takes about a decade of wild blue dancing to shed just one. If we are lucky and if we dance hard enough, will we be able to look each other in the eye, our faces clear, between us nothing but air?

And what do we do with the nets, the sails that luffed, that tangled around our feet? What do we do with the knowledge and the anger?

I see the veils twisted, knotted between us like sheets for escape. The taut material is strong when pulled and thinned to ropes between us. Primary cords. We can use the means and symbol of our long histories, as women, of emotional and intellectual incarceration. We can remove the flimsy shadows from before our faces and braid them into ropes. We can fasten the ropes between us so that if one of us slips, as we climb, as we live, there are others in line to stand firm, to bear her up, to be her witnesses and anchors.

—LOUISE ERDRICH

20

VISIBILITY

You who do not remember
passage from the other world
I tell you I could speak again: whatever
returns from oblivion returns
to find a voice:
from the center of my life came
a great fountain, deep blue
shadows on azure seawater.

—LOUISE GLUCK, "The Wild Iris"

WHEN I WAS A CHILD, I longed for invisibility. The appeal was power, I believe, the power to belong without being required to participate, to escape judgment but to retain the opportunity to learn.

I learned that shame was behind this desire after rape brought me a load so staggering I had to pay attention. Shame grew out of my initial quiet, my desire not to tell, to pretend that rape had not occurred. In this privatizing of grief, I confused the *experience* with the *responsibility*.

This is an intuitive choice, and one of the reasons why victims of shameful crimes choose invisibility. When the victim is the only one visible, others may attach the shame of that crime to the victim.

"She will find," writes Andrea Dworkin in "A Battered Wife Survives," "that her parents, doctors, the police, her best friend, the neighbors upstairs and across the hall and next door, all despise the woman who cannot keep her own house in order, her injuries hidden, her despair to herself, her smile amiable and convincing."

There's a time and a place for feeling like a victim, for example, when one's participation is coerced by force. In these cases, the more a victim's powerlessness is recognized, the less shame is attached to the experience. This is the most powerful help one can give the victim of a shameful crime.

I was fortunate that by 1981 aspects of the culture could support this idea. "Not until the women's liberation movement of the 1970s was it recognized that the most common post-traumatic disorders are not those of men in war but of women in civilian life," writes Judith Herman. The first rape speak-out was held in New York in 1971, the same year that the first rape crisis center opened in the United States.

Remaining in the role of the victim is dangerous, though, if for no other reason than that it is a waste of human resources. The people most able to change the world are those motivated by inside knowledge. *You who see, tell the others.* In the case of rape, this means survivors and those men and women who are close to them.

Judith Herman writes that real recovery from the isolation of trauma comes only when "the survivor comes to understand the issues of principle that transcend her personal grievance against the perpetrator . . . [a] principle of social justice that connects the fate of others to her own." Becoming visible in some way as a survivor makes that connection, and also remakes the world for the children being born to inherit it.

Virginia Woolf raised the question of how the world's literature might have been enriched if Shakespeare had had a "wonderfully gifted sister," and she'd had a room of her own. I wonder about the silence of Scheherazade's daughters. What might the world be like if they told all their stories?

THE SUMMER OF 1990 was terrible for women in Minnesota. Between June and August of that year, ten women were murdered in acts of domestic violence. A doctor's wife was shot in the head by her husband while she held her seven-year-old son by the hand. A thirty-five-year-old woman had her throat slashed as she arrived for work at the Hennepin County Government Center, where she'd filed for an order of protection the day before.

That fall, a group of writers and visual artists found their lunchtime conversations at the Minneapolis College of Art and Design full of the lingering effect of these murders. They began to talk, casually, then with deliberation, about doing something.

I knew the women in this group and admired them for the project they were hatching, but nothing in me called out to join them. I tend to prefer rumination over action. In the fall of 1990, I was teaching, I was in therapy a few times a week, I was mothering a three-year-old. Tim and I were preparing to separate. I was *busy*.

In early December, I had a morning at home to sit in the weak sunshine, drinking tea and reading the paper, and there it was again, headline news. A mother of four had been killed by a former boyfriend, her body found by her six-year-old son. Downstairs, sleeping on the couch, her sister had also been murdered. The wail of these deaths was suddenly audible, and I couldn't stand it. I couldn't go about my business, couldn't abide the din. I needed help. I called my friend Jill, who was involved in the project. *Did you read about the murders? I need to do something. Is there something I can do?*

• • •

A FEW MONTHS LATER, our group completed work on the project we called the Silent Witnesses: twenty-six life-size wooden figures representing the Minnesota women killed in domestic violence in 1990. The figures were painted fire-engine red—no features, just the flat outline of women's bodies, simple as paper dolls. The genius of the Witnesses' design is the fact that they take up space. It's been said that this is art's function, "to make the invisible visible."

Each of the figures bears a name and the story of that particular woman's death. This was my part in the project. The information was gathered by the Minnesota Coalition for Battered Women, a nonprofit service group and the only agency interested enough in the deaths to be keeping track. Working with the grim document they compiled, I saw that "keeping track" is a critical step for change. Without the details, a problem easily remains hidden.

Their method was simple. They read the papers. They were quick to caution us that their numbers were certainly low. We added a twenty-seventh figure, the Uncounted Woman, to represent those women whose deaths had not been acknowledged. From this list, Patricia and I wrote the stories that were affixed on small gold shields over the hearts of the Witnesses.

> She lived in Little Falls. She died of multiple blows to the head. She had bruises on her face and upper body and was identified through dental records. The man with whom she shared an apartment was charged with second-degree murder in her death.

Patricia and I wrote the stories one long winter afternoon. We were unprepared for the spiritual gravity of the task, beginning like busy writers with a job to do. We finished feeling as if we'd slipped onto Charon's boat and drifted into an intimate acquaintance with evil.

What had these women been like? What pride and what love had framed the borders of their lives? Eventually we reconciled ourselves to the fact that we would never know. And so we told the stories of the deaths of twenty-six women ranging in age from sixteen to eighty-six. Each entry began with the word *she* because, whatever the circumstances of her life, each had been killed because she was a *she*.

> She was the mother of two children. She lived in Parkers Prairie. She was shot in the head by her husband, who then committed suicide. She survived for two days. Her children, ages 5 and 9, were home at the time of the shooting and survive her.

There's a strange transmogrification that occurs when the Witnesses are visible in a room. All those who work with them speak of it. You begin to call them by name: Kate, Rita, Sigrid, Carmen, Rose. You are careful not to jostle them, to handle their sturdy wooden bodies gingerly. When all twenty-seven are standing together, in a church basement, a student union, or a corporate lunchroom, there is a presence in the room, detectable, like breath. "When we first set them up on their stands, I thought what a party we'd be having if they were alive," said a woman who helped create the Witnesses.

WOMEN COME TO THE CAPITOL is an annual event in Minnesota that gathers advocacy groups together to lobby for women's issues. In 1991, it was also the occasion for the Silent Witnesses' first appearance. The red figures of the murdered women stood behind the speakers, perfectly fulfilling the destiny of their naming. Sen. Paul Wellstone addressed the group, accompanied by his wife, Sheila, who never forgot her first view of the Witnesses. She later became their powerful representative as she worked to bring attention to domestic violence in Minnesota. In 1995, she brought the Silent Witnesses to Washington, D.C., for the first time, where they were viewed by legislators debating the 1995 crime bill.

At the end of that February morning, sixty women gathered to march the figures across the street and into the capitol rotunda. In the bustle of preparation, a volunteer preparing to carry a Witness turned to see a young woman at her elbow. *Do you mind if I carry this figure?* the woman asked. *She was my sister.*

Thus began a series of connections between the Witnesses and those who mourned the murdered women as friends and family and coworkers and neighbors. So, too, were strangers brought into the circle of grief, their encounters with the Witnesses shoring up a decision to leave an abusive partner or granting the courage to speak to a frightened, silenced friend before it was too late.

The Witnesses remained at the rotunda a full week, startling the lobbyists and pages and senators and security guards who stopped to read their stories. At the end of that first day, exhilarated and exhausted, I sat for a moment in a friend's car. Most of the women who had worked on the project had some personal experience with domestic violence. I did not. Why had my work on this project been so personally stirring?

Then it hit me, a hot thought in the February dusk. At this point, I was still keeping quiet about the night I nearly lost my life to sexual violence. Sitting in the car, I remembered how it felt to know I was going to die, to envision my body being found in a pool of blood. I remembered my fury that I would not be able to *tell* anyone what had happened.

With the Silent Witness project, we *told* what had happened to Nicole and to Barbara and to Bethany and to Helen. The moment of their deaths had been noticed. More than that, their deaths were helping to make visible a crime wave so out of control it is the most common cause of injury to women in America.

In October of 1997, as I was finishing this book, I joined thousands of people in Washington, D.C., for the first national Silent Witness March. Fueled by the dedication of Janet Hagberg, an originator of the Minnesota project, the march signified the spread of the Silent Witness Project to all fifty states in just seven years. To the lilt and moan of bagpipes, fifteen hundred Witnesses were marched in a resolute red line from the foot of the Washington Monument to the steps of the Capitol.

That day in Washington is a new favorite in my life. In the evening, when the Witnesses stood around the Capitol reflecting pool, they made a staggering swash of testimony. By their absence they are present, all the women we've lost. I returned from the march with an image for the refusal to disappear. *We are still here. Now that you see us, what will you do?* Moving from one to the next to the next to read their stories, I saw how terribly similar they were and how heartbreaking in their particulars. So many died in the presence of their children; so many of their children were present with us in Washington.

And Andre was there with me. I wanted him to see the power that an image has in carrying the news. The breathtaking dignity of the truth. And I wanted him to hear my voice declare with the bagpipes my gratitude for my life, for it led me to him.

At the end of his defining memoir of grief, *Heaven's Coast*, Mark Dody makes a list of consolations. *Metaphor, the present, bitterness, Aretha Franklin, longing, dogs,* he writes. I would add poetry, the garden, revenge, and my son. These are the things that helped. During the worst days, Andre was the light in the house. Sometimes the demands of caring for him, the imperative to be alert, interested, cheerful even, seemed too difficult. In fact, they urged me on when otherwise I might have submitted too easily to the consolation of bitterness. I came to count on the new life we were making to enliven my countenance. Because he expected laughter and adventure, there we were, having it.

When a soul is lost, it is in need of others. This is what we mean by *help*—a listening ear, a place to rest, a story, a carriage lined with sugared cakes. Accepting help begins with being visible. But the end of the story, I believe, is using visibility as a form of power.

LESLIE MARMON SILKO tells the story of a tricky curve in the road on the reservation where she grew up. Drivers who take the curve too fast are likely to end up in a small ravine that drops off right below a popular roadhouse. She speaks of the ritual of reassurance that occurs whenever a car goes down the ravine. Everyone comes out of the bar to tell of the time they missed the curve, the time their brother went over the hill. They are a small tribe, she says, and it's important that no one be lost to shame or the mistaken notion that they alone have blundered. Stories keep everyone in the circle.

One night at a gathering of friends, shortly after the first anniversary, Jim handed me a poem he'd written. It was a nearly casual moment, the typed page folded in quarters, but reading it changed everything. "Details from the August Heat: Your Rape One Year Later," it said at the top of the page.

In 1982 the word *rape* rarely appeared in the newspapers, let alone in art, in conversation. I stared at the letters on the page, surprised, immediately comforted, aware that this was an exceptional moment. I might say that the feeling was of being returned to the circle.

In 1975, when Susan Brownmiller published her ground-breaking study of the history and sociology of rape, *Against Our Will*, rape at last entered the cultural conversation. But not for long. Even today, her book is one of a handful on the subject designed for wide readership. Though courageous and epic in scope, it did not speak a personal word. It was not what I needed then.

I was looking for someone to name what had happened to me. Without this naming, I remained alone with a terrible knowledge. Art can do this work. The story and the image can carry us until we find our footing. The poems and words of others that I have included in this book were consolations, part of the ballast that stabilized me through the sad years, that told me someone was paying attention, could see me, and would not turn away.

Details from the August Heat:
Your Rape One Year Later

The unripe tomato left to sun
on the garbage can lid, the tight
yellow wax of its waiting, the gourd pitched
sideways, unbalanced, its sickly green
looks weakened, the color of a lime
held under water. Slick with August dew,
this day must also begin for you.

One year ago today, you woke, in darkness,
to a new, less complicated life. A knife
at your throat, a man unbalanced, slick
with that addiction: not to you,
but to your life, submerged, blurred
beyond all recognition. Not to you,
but for your absolute, unwavering attention.

Tiger lilies have a way of hiding out
against garage doors, brick walls, or a gray
fencepost. My old landlord keeps them for his wife,
dead three years. To whom he sings each night,
playing badly on the mandolin. Music
is at least a fan: the sorrow pushes
at a curtain, touches a face, rearranges the invisible

helpless air. "Well, now you'll have
something to write about," that young man said, then
raped you. "Details," you wrote me once,
"those are the things which can be said,
huge and neglected." The next day
you left that place for good. You found a house
with double locks, a yard, a suburb far away.

And then the nights began to make you pay.
Terror is boring, each night the same ritual:
he is back inside the house, making his way slowly,
cut by cut, into your waiting life. You are certain
that you will always wake like this, forced
to be what he must have, again and again. His face
will never end. His jittery way with words. His steady,
        gloved hands.

The old man has a secret: water
every night after dark. A pool of black water
under each stake. He says
that's what it takes for tomatoes *like this:*

he makes a circle gesture meaning perfect.
Perfect is a full night's sleep.

You will lean up against it, a gray fencepost,
and one night it will hold.
This day waits for you, huge
and neglected. You will not forget
where you have been and what was done
upon you. Details from the August heat:
grapes ease their way from green to purple, you
work all day then turn to children's stories.

Once upon a time, the large print reads,
and the words glide by
like illustrated days in a bedtime fairy tale.

      —JIM MOORE

21

BEDTIME STORY/4

"THE SNOW QUEEN"

The Sixth Part

The Lapland Woman and the Finland Woman

Sofi and Andre sit on the floor while I read, since there's not space for all of us on the bed anymore. Andre's room is packed with relics from the days when we began this story—stuffed animals, dinosaur posters, rocks, and his collection of miniature wizards and warriors.

On his bookcase is a photograph I love. He's midleap in an ocean wave, his arms flung out in amazement. I took it on a Florida island the winter that his father and I were divorced. All week he leapt like a sprite, shouting with every wave. He is a remarkable boy to me. I worry over his spirit like it's a struggling fire, but he's ablaze with enthusiasm, helpless with goofy laughter, undaunted by the kind of bravery his life requires of him.

"So, if you remember, Gerda had just set out with the reindeer to go to Lapland, right?"

Sofi smiles, remembering our joke.

The pair stop first at the cottage of a Lapp woman. *The reindeer told her the whole of Gerda's story, but he told his own first, for that seemed to be much more important.* She tells them they must travel four hundred more miles to Finmark. She writes a message on a dried codfish to send along to her friend there, who reads the codfish, eats it, then listens to both stories. The reindeer asks the Finnish woman to give Gerda the strength of twelve men, so she can complete the journey.

I can't give her greater power than she has already! Can't you see how great that is? Can't you see how she makes man and beast serve her, and how well she's made her way in the world on her own bare feet? She musn't know of her power from us—it comes from her heart.

I love this passage where Gerda gets her due, where Andersen comes out and tells us it's persistence that is heroic.

"What's a codfish?" Sofi wrinkles her nose.

"Hey, she's hungry," says Andre. He's beside me now, still willing to be physically close. "*Living snowflakes shaped like hedgehogs?*" he declaims, reading ahead over my shoulder. In the years it's taken to get through this story, he's learned to read.

The Finnish woman instructs the reindeer to carry Gerda to the edge of the Snow Queen's garden and leave her by the bush with the red berries. Gerda makes her way toward the palace, where she encounters great, living snowflakes shaped like hedgehogs and masses of snakes knotted together, darting their heads out.

But as she utters a prayer, her breath takes the shape of angels armed for combat who pierce the snowflakes with their spears and move her toward the palace.

. . .

"THE SNOW QUEEN"

The Seventh Part

What Happened in the Snow Queen's Palace, and What Happened Afterwards

Inside the palace, whose walls were made of snow and whose doors and windows were cutting wind, there is no joy.

Gaiety never came this way, no, not so much as a little dance for the bears, with the gale blowing up and the polar-bears walking on their hind-legs and showing their fine manners; never a little card-party with slap-your-mouth and strike-your-paw; never a little bit of fun over coffee for the young white-fox ladies—empty, vast, and cold it was in the Snow Queen's halls.

A man sits with us and listens tonight. He's coming in on the end of this story, but he's interested in how it turns out. *Not so much as a little dance for the bears, never a little bit of fun over coffee for the young white-fox ladies,* he repeats.

I smile at him. These phrases will become part of our language now.

In the center of the palace lies a frozen lake called The Mirror of Intelligence, broken into a thousand pieces shaped exactly alike. Kay spends his days arranging the pieces into patterns, trying to spell the word eternity. The Snow Queen promises him the whole world and a new pair of skates, if he can so arrange the pieces.

When Gerda enters the palace, the Snow Queen is away. Gerda finds Kay dragging pieces of ice about. Kay does not recognize her until she cries, and her hot tears melt his frozen heart. When he weeps, the grain of glass falls out of his eye, and the two friends dance until they are tired. Even the ice fragments feel their happiness and dance, coming to rest in the shape of the letters that spell eternity.

Andre is yawning when I look up from the book, so tired at the end of his busy days he sometimes falls asleep without a story. "We're almost done, but we don't want to leave out the happy ending," I say with the smile that tells him I'm up to something.

He looks at me to assess my playful mood. "There's always a happy ending in these stories," he says with worldly confidence.

"Exactly. Happiness is always a good place to stop."

Gerda and Kay make their way back to the reindeer, who has been joined by a doe *whose udders were full, and she gave the children her warm milk and kissed them on the lips.*

The reindeer carries them back to the Finnish woman, who makes them warm, and then back to the Lapp woman, who gives them clothes and a sled. On their way south, they pass the robber-girl driving the golden coach. She tells them what has become of the prince and the princess, and all about the death of the crow. Finally they arrive home as the world returns to spring.

They went up the stairs and into the living room, where everything stood in the same place as before, and the clock said Tick! Tock! and the hands turned round. But as they entered the door they realized that they had grown up. . . . There they sat together, grown up, yet children still, children at heart—and it was summer, warm and beautiful summer.

22

THE LAUREL TREE

I part the outthrusting
branches and come in
beneath
the blessed and the
blessing trees.
Though I am silent
there is singing around me
Though I am dark
there is vision around me
Though I am heavy
there is flight around me

—WENDELL BERRY

Rows and rows and rows of color where we walk. Tea roses, hybrids, the Peace rose, which smells sultry, climbing reds, the pure whites I always bend to. We started with roses, roses on my door, then a walk in the Lake Harriet Rose Garden on a burnished fall day. I hesitated and then I took his hand. We come back to the Rose Garden now as if it belongs to us, as if the other gazers and strolling couples are invisible.

. . .

Wʜᴀᴛ ɪs ɪᴛ we need from the wild, from the wooded, crawling, humming life that goes on without us, yet to which we each feel privately related? There is, first of all, beauty. To be smitten by the light through the old pines, the wild trillium, a black band of fur caterpilling across the path, is essentially a matter of destiny. However long it may take us to find it, we are born for this rapture.

And then there is the ability of a pond, or a meadow, or a mountain perch to shout down the chatter of our complicated minds and tune us to the steady song we've improvised since birth. Somehow this native sound comes naturally to the surface when we're alone and in the company of trees or desert sand. "With common sense, the park saves lives and sanity," said one commentator in a radio broadcast about Central Park.

Sʜᴇ ᴡᴀs ᴇxᴀᴄᴛʟʏ my age. I reacted to the news of her death as if in response to a bond between us. A bond, it could be argued, that exists among all women; one we try not to notice. Someone murdered Maria Isabel Pinto Montero Alves, a forty-four-year-old Brazilian woman, in Central Park in September 1995. Her body was found 350 yards from the site of the 1989 beating and rape of the woman who became known as "the Central Park Jogger." In June 1996, another woman will be found in Central Park near Summit Rock, beaten, the victim of an attempted rape.

Alves was a regular jogger in Central Park, often beginning as early as four-thirty in the morning in order to arrive on time for her job as a clerk in a shoe store. Her mother, when she arrived from Rio de Janeiro to claim her daughter's body, described Maria's early morning runs as "gaining strength from nature." My outrage at her murder registers first as blame. She should never have *been* in the park at that hour, I hear myself thinking. In fact, she should never have been *murdered* in the park.

The walls around Central Park define it as a protected place, a respite. Its existence speaks of a society that "gained strength from nature" even as it grew into a city, but I have always viewed the gates of Central Park with a Gothic apprehension. *Cross here at your own risk, silly girl,* they say, and the carriages and fountains and zoos for children seem a clever disguise papering over the real character of the urban park. This might just be the view of a midwesterner on the occasional visit. Nevertheless, it is a female grief that we enter the garden at our own peril.

Our feet are not bound, but we act either out of defiance or recklessness when we run the darkened path. Many of us learn to live without the relief of trees or a night walk when the snow is tumbling down. We are afraid or afraid of being afraid. When fear confined me to solitude in interior spaces, I began to lose access to a windy, open quality in my spirit. It is a female grief.

FOUR YEARS AFTER I was raped, I spent a week at an estate in Lake Forest, Illinois, that had been transformed into a working retreat for artists and writers. Out behind the house, the land stretches for forty acres. First, there is a garden, the crooked trees loaded with blushing apples; the dahlias, tall as sunflowers, nodding before cosmos and phlox; then prairie, with feathery grasses moving like water in the wind; then woods, then a thicker woods cut by a stream, part of a parcel of land donated to the Nature Conservancy.

Perhaps three days into my stay, I found myself on my knees in the far woods. The yellow milk of the sun streamed onto the patch of leaves and needles where I succumbed to the arching branches, the smell of loam, the white butterflies. I was alone in the woods for the first time in years. I'd fought off twinges of panic as I headed out from the house, but I silenced my fears with the words, *this is private property.*

Then, I did an uncharacteristic thing. I spoke a vow. *If I ever have enough money, I'll make a place like this for women.* A place where women collared by fear can walk and let beauty hold them up. A place both protected and wild. Though I am no longer afraid to be alone in our only world, there remains from this moment a belief that a walled garden for women is a necessary idea. Every day, there are women falling to their knees for the need of such relief.

On the North Shore of Lake Superior, just before the Pigeon River marks the end of the United States, is the Grand Portage Indian Reservation. A cedar tree, known popularly as the Witch Tree and more properly as the Ma-ni-do Gee-zhi-gance or Spirit Little Cedar Tree, twists out of a rocky outcropping there like a sentinel. It is thought to be more than four hundred years old and has long been a sacred place for the Anishinabe people.

I was drawn by descriptions of the famous tree's ability to grow straight up out of craggy rock with no visible means of sustenance. I liked the metaphor in that, the implication that survival, even glory, is possible under conditions of extremity. I wanted to see the tree but never made the effort required to travel that far up the North Shore.

Then, I heard it was too late. Vandalism and an increased number of tourists had caused the Grand Portage Tribal Government to restrict access to the tree. Nevertheless, when I found myself in Grand Portage for the first time, I made inquiries. I was told I'd have to "see Melvin" about that.

"We're not going there to see something," Melvin told my friend and me. "We're going there to learn something." Melvin said this more than once, and each time I missed his meaning. I wanted to see the tree. If Melvin also wanted me to learn something, well, fine.

A solemn man in his thirties, he asked a question or two, then led us to a sterile conference room at the Grand Portage Lodge and Casino where he readied himself to make what looked like a well-rehearsed presentation. He didn't answer my question: Can we see the Witch Tree? He asked us to agree not to interrupt him until he finished speaking. An hour later, after visual aids, philosophical declarations, poetry, maps, a history of the Reservation and eventually of the Spirit Cedar, we were allowed to speak.

During Melvin's presentation, which was stiff and obscure in many spots, my friend and I caught each other's eye in bemused panic. We seemed to have gotten ourselves trapped in a tedious lecture with no end in sight. Later that day, he did take us to see the Spirit Cedar, and my friend and I spent the next few days wandering among the waterfalls and mountain peaks of the Anishinabe land, seeing the full range of the reservation's beauty. He said, "Don't come here just to see the tree. Come for the land." He said, "We're not going there to *see* something; we're going there to *learn* something."

Afterward we walked back to the road through a spirited birch forest, the wreck and tumble of uncleared land. Ferns like dense cobwebs made the trees look bearded, something out of a fairy tale. What had I learned? As Melvin drove us home, the sun setting purple on the fearsome lake, what stayed with me was the way he spoke of his people's dilemma. His words seemed to address the question behind every line in this book: *How do we protect what we love? Can there be safety without constriction? Fearlessness without recklessness?*

"If you put fences up around it or guards in front of it, it can't fulfill its nature," Melvin said. "You have to protect it with love and patience and understanding." Melvin had assigned himself that job—educating visitors, one and two at a time. "People run in here and say, 'Hey, I've got fifteen minutes and I want to see the tree.'" He's kind enough not to look me in the eye as he says this. We both know that though I was willing to sit through his lecture, my toes were tapping.

"It's not something to grab, to possess," he said. "It exists for its own purposes in context with everything else that is here. Its beauty and power are increased by this, but it requires a shift in point of view."

What remained for me from my visit to the Spirit Cedar was an approach to the idea of protection. I don't want fences and guards—the fear that warps one's true nature—but a world that takes seriously my need for freedom and safety. If we put our trust in community, then we must have a community we can trust. This requires a shift in point of view. Women's beauty and sexuality exist *for their own purpose in context with everything else.* Fear can smolder a long time under the surface of functional lives. When women no longer inhabit their bodies, we miss them. Sometimes, we lose them.

It's probably been done—A Life of the Body, Memoirs of a Torso, The Autobiography of My Flesh and Bones. I'm in a new chapter, too busy to take notes. Awareness brings pleasure, hunger, and desire. Mornings when I wake and find I am not alone, I feel near tears, as if I'd had a close call, barely escaped with my life. My body elongates, relaxes, curls toward the man who wakes grinning. There are long stretches of peace. There are roses, red and yellow and pale like the lip of a shell. There is life as always, and a new way of life.

I can't help looking back over my shoulder. How powerfully my body has shaped my life. Winter came and there was such a frozen time when the rosebushes were buried and nothing, it seemed, could be revived. A long journey back, but not back to the same place.

The sand is firm and damp from the morning's rain. It feels like sugar. It's warm with summer. Blades of grass tip toward me holding rain. Every clover flower has its bee, its striped yellow moth. This moth I'm watching seems, just now, more important than anything I might wish or say.

Here's my feeling about Eden: it was a garden and we were in it and of it and we still are. There are snakes in the garden and apples. This knowledge should not cast us out of paradise but enable us to stay there, together. We may need walls or shoes. But *knowledge* of evil is a force for good.

It was in a garden that I told my son I had survived a rape before he was born. These were words I never wanted to say, though I knew the day would come. I would not have chosen this time or the occasion, but in the end, I felt peaceful with this knowledge between us.

We were together on an island in Lake Michigan, one of those wild and protected places where I have written so much of this book. We were at the end of a long, happy day in the company of loved ones. I had work to do, a deadline to meet. Andre had been outside playing catch, and he drifted inside to hang his arms around my neck. Idly, I acknowledged him but kept typing, forgetting, as I still sometimes do, that he reads everything now.

In a still, shocked voice he asked, "Is *that* what your book is about?"

Oddly, the subject of rape had arisen just a few days before. A story on the radio told about the Mike Tyson/Evander Holyfield fight in which Tyson bit off a portion of Holyfield's ear. I'd muttered something about Tyson being a troubled man who'd already been to prison for a violent crime.

"What'd he do?" Andre asked as he drank his juice.

I drew a breath, considered fudging, then decided this was knowledge he would need, knowledge it was my place to impart. "Do you know the meaning of the word *rape*?"

He nodded, looking directly at me.

"What does it mean?" I asked.

I find his answer eerie in retrospect. At the time, I was just trying to get through the moment. "It's when someone breaks into your house and makes you have sex," he said, uncomfortable with the words.

"That's right, though rape can happen anywhere. It's a crime no matter where it happens."

I stood and put my arm around him, and we walked outside into our friends' rock garden. We sat in the grass in the early evening sun and talked. Our conversation was simple and brief, the way Andre prefers it. I told him it had been hard. He asked me if I'd been hurt. I told him I'd had a lot of help and that I was all right. I told him that I'd learned from the experience, learned about how to accept my biggest feelings, how to ask for help, how to find my courage. He told me he was sorry. He seemed a full human being in that moment, a young man.

AT THE WEST END of the island in Rainy Lake where I write these last words stands a cedar tree. Years ago, I was mesmerized by the light reflecting off the rolling waves and flickering across the lower boughs. It seemed I was seeing the pulsating spirit of the tree itself. Today, I swim beneath that tree with a woman whose infectious laugh crackles the air. The light animates the cedar tree exactly as it did in what seems a gone and distant life.

I've marked this fifteenth anniversary privately, in the company of women, on this island up at the end of the country. My dreams have been quirky and mild. In my heart there is wild love for a good man. I'm at home in my skin, warmed by the August sun, cleaned out by the edge of winter in the wind. I push off into the cold black water and swim for the rocky shore of the next island.

NOTES

Lexicon

Definitions from *American Heritage Dictionary, 3rd ed.*, Houghton Mifflin, 1992.

Prologue

Extrapolating from the 1990 National Victim Center study and interviews with a sampling of more than nine hundred women, researcher Diana Russell estimates a rape-survivor population in the United States of between 12 and 41 million. The FBI's *Uniform Crime Report* estimates 1.5 million reported rapes between 1972 and 1991. Using their estimate that only one in six rapes are reported, the twenty-year figure rises to 12 million.

Chapter 1: Bedtime Story / 1

Italicized portions of "The Snow Queen" are quoted from a translation from the Danish by L. W. Kingsland in *Hans Andersen's Fairy Tales: A Selection*, Oxford University Press, 1959. Roman text is my summary based on this translation.

Chapter 6: After

I have relied heavily on material from Dr. Judith Herman's important and affirming research as it is presented in *Trauma and Recovery*, Basic Books, 1992.

Chapter 7: Exodus

The Susan Griffin quote is from *Rape: The Politics of Consciousness*, Harper & Row, 1986.

The Andrea Dworkin quote is from *Intercourse*, Free Press, 1987.

For information about "Until Someone Wakes Up," conceived and originally directed by Carolyn Levy and written by Carolyn Levy, Laura Bradley, C. Todd Griffin, Marcy Laughinghouse, David Page, Josh Schultz, Debra Sengupta, Elizabeth J. Wood, and Cara McChegney, et al., contact Carolyn c/o Hamline University, St. Paul, Minnesota 55104; 651-523-2972. An essay by Levy about the collaboration is included in the ground-breaking anthology *Transforming a Rape Culture*, edited by Emilie Buchwald, Pamela Fletcher, and Martha Roth, Milkweed Editions, 1993.

Chapter 9: Fear

For an analysis of the social and psychological effects that the fear of rape has on American women, see *The Female Fear: The Social Cost of Rape*, Margaret T. Gordon and Stephanie Riger, University of Illinois Press, 1991.

"How I Walk" is from Deborah Keenan's *Happiness*, Coffee House Press, 1995.

Chapter 11: Roots of Fear

The exact quote is from Balzac. "One cannot thread a needle when the needle doesn't stand still." This phrase was commonly used by defense lawyers before rape laws were reformed in the 1970s. Under the old definitions, women were required to prove they had resisted a rape by showing evidence of a physical injury.

Chapter 12: Do I *Look* Angry?

The Andrea Dworkin quote is from "Violence Against Women: It Breaks the Heart, Also the Bones" included in *Letters from the War Zone*, Lawrence Hill Books, 1993.

Chapter 14: Love, Labor, Loss

The "lines of the poet" are from "Lucky Life" by Gerald Stern. *Rebounding from Childbirth* by Lynn Madsen, Bergin & Garvey, 1994.

Chapter 16: Your Aura's Got Holes in It

"Gretel from a sudden clearing" is from *The Good Thief* by Marie Howe, Persea Books, 1988.

Chapter 19: Justice

For more detail on the research of Peggy Reeves Sanday, see *A Woman Scorned*, Doubleday, 1996. Also by Sanday and Ruth Gallagher Goodenough, *Beyond the Second Sex: New Directions in the Anthropology of Gender*, University of Pennsylvania Press, 1990.

The full text of "The Veils" by Louise Erdrich is included in *Transforming a Rape Culture*, edited by Emilie Buchwald, Pamela Fletcher, and Martha Roth, Milkweed Editions, 1992.

Chapter 20: Visibility

For more information about the Silent Witness National Initiative, contact Janet Hagberg and Jane Zeller at 550 Rice Street, Saint Paul, MN 55103.

The Andrea Dworkin quote is from "A Battered Wife Survives" included in *Letters from a War Zone*, Lawrence Hill Books, 1993.

Marisha Chamberlain considers the "Scheherazade impulse" in her full-length play, *Scheherazade*, which centers around a woman's conversation with a rapist, Dramatists Play Service, 1985.

Among the consolations I identified was revenge, as in "the only revenge is a happy life."

"Details from the August Heat" is from *The Freedom of History* by Jim Moore, Milkweed Editions, 1988.

ACKNOWLEDGMENTS

During the seven years I worked on this book, many people contributed their energy to bolster my heart and spirit, encouraging me to walk forward while looking backward. I thank you all. And I thank here, in particular, those who contributed to its writing. I am grateful to Joan Drury and Kelly Kager of Norcroft, the Mallard Island Foundation, Pamela Holt, Jane Johnston, and the White Hotel for offering spaces with the long horizon of open water that I craved while working on *Telling*. The financial support of the National Endowment for the Arts, the Bush Foundation, The Loft, and the McKnight Foundation was crucial for the completion of this book.

I thank Philip Lopate and Rosellen Brown for their potent encouragement. Brigitte Frase, Patricia Kirkpatrick, Julie Landsman, Todd Maitland, Cheri Register, and Bart Schneider were my first audience, reading early drafts and challenging me with questions and suggestions.

The unflagging support of Deborah Keenan and Mary Francois Rockcastle, wise readers and companions in happiness, was tangible sustenance in the darkest times. Enduring gratitude to Jim Moore for his dedication to lunch and literature and friendship. A wide grin for the Babes in the Woods and particularly my thanks to Danielle Sosin for our partnership in writing by water. I'm thankful to Ellie Winninghoff for our late-night talks, and to Anastasia Faunce for the illuminating conversation.

Additionally, I want to thank JoAnn Verberg for having art history at her fingertips and leading me to the Bernini sculptures, and Eric Utne for his way with titles. My appreciation to Jeanne Farrar and Ben Shank for their perceptive support during the

Baugh trial. Brimming thanks to Marion Moore and Louise Erdrich, angels of delivery.

I am indebted to my agent, Ellen Levine, for her enthusiasm from the first and patience to the last. Diane Reverand gave this book meticulous editorial attention and has blessed me with the invigorating confidence of her belief.

Finally, to Larry LaVercombe, who read every page with his heart open and his mind alive to what is true about hope. For his faith in me, for abundant love in a late season, for trips to the copy store and the Web page, for his passionate belief that art can do work in the world. My love.

• • •

For information and conversation visit the
Telling Web page:

www.tellingofrape.com